THE TRUTH ABOUT ESP

Books by Hans Holzer

HANS HOLZER

The Truth
About ESP.

WHAT IT IS,
HOW IT WORKS,
AND HOW YOU DEVELOP IT

Doubleday & Company, Inc., Garden City, New York, 1974

133.8
H

ISBN: 0-385-05253-7
Library of Congress Catalog Card Number 73–11709

CONTENTS

INTRODUCTION

Ever since Dr. Joseph B. Rhine made the term ESP popular, people have been wondering whether or not there is such a thing as extrasensory perception. Back in the 1930s Professor Rhine taught parapsychology at Duke University. The term parapsychology is the creation of the "father of psychical research" in this country, Professor Rhine. It means the study of those phenomena which are presently outside the reaches of ordinary psychology, but which may someday be within the limits of psychology. ESP stands for extrasensory perception and refers to the ability by a person to perceive beyond the limits of the ordinary five senses, as we know them. In *ESP and You* I wrote, "Everybody has an extra sense beyond the five normally relied upon, but only a minority of people are aware of it and an even smaller percentage knows how to use this sixth sense to good advantage." I also held that the nature of ESP is both spontaneous and unexpected and consequently cannot be reproduced at will in a laboratory. "Conditions beyond your knowledge make the experience possible, and you have no control over it. The sole exception is the art of proper thinking— the training toward the wider use of your own ESP powers." Since the publication of that book I have learned much more about the nature of ESP in man and animals. Although I have not changed my conviction that it is in fact a natural part of human nature and inborn in all of us, I have come to define it somewhat differently. There is no such thing as a sixth sense, separate from the five ordinary senses. There are, however, instances where the so-called ordinary five senses do not suffice to explain certain phenomena taking place in the mind of a subject or between more than one subject. What we have come to call ESP, then, is not a separate sense at all but an extension of the ordinary five senses beyond what we used to consider their limitations but which in fact are not. If anything, man has five extra senses. I also feel that the so-called ordinary five senses are merely different expressions of the sensory apparatus of man and thus not separate expressions at all but parts of one's over-all faculty. Under those circumstances, the ESP factor is merely an extension into another band of that one and only human faculty and not a mysterious outside force open only to a small number of special people, perhaps those born with a caul over their face or in some other fashion rewarded by fate. Extrasensory perception is a natural faculty; the lack of that ability or the indifference toward its use found in large segments of the population are unnatural expressions in man: since everyone has ESP, those who do not seem to be aware of their faculty are either ignoring it, suppressing it, or have ascribed certain ESP phenomena in their lives to other causes. In particular, the habit of dismissing ESP phenomena as coincidental, accidental, imaginary, hallucinatory, or, if all else fails, as probably meaningless and worthless is a widespread way in which the average materialist likes to eliminate the presence of

ESP in his or her person. This allows him to stay within his preconceived and securely cemented philosophy, a world in which everything obeys the law of cause and effect and there is nothing more beyond. Such an artificially restricted world is of course at variance with the facts found by science in the universe around us; but as yet there are millions of human beings who prefer the self-imposed prison of a partial and strongly biased philosophy to the excitement and adventure of a wider world in which all things are possible, though many things are not yet fully understood.

Among the things that many people have as yet not fully grasped are the phenomena generally classified as extrasensory perception. This appears to be the result of faulty education and of antiquated values; modern science is far from a purveyor of miracles; in fact, modern science is letting us down badly in more and more instances. But the acceptance of an "obstructed universe," even though there are continual signs that this does not correspond to fact, is a coward's way of coping with the puzzles of nature. If the facts presented by parapsychology, if the phenomena classed as ESP are true and real, then the old order of things is not. If what I say in these pages, and what others in the field of parapsychology have said elsewhere, corresponds to generally valid conditions, there is an urgent need to re-evaluate the postulations of the past. The law of cause and effect is no longer the only rule by which the universe operates. Even Dr. Carl Jung, the eminent psychiatrist, and his "law of meaningful coincidence" or acausal synchronicity are not the final answers to the problem at hand: beyond these two relationships there is a third superior order of things, the law by which the universe operates in and through man and all things, whether living or not. That law, which I must call for want of a better name, the Universal Law, is the basis upon which the facts of ESP can be understood and studied. Once we realize that ESP phenomena obey specific and comparatively simple laws even though these laws differ greatly from our earthbound laws of cause and effect, then we also come to understand why ESP phenomena can so easily circumvent orthodox concepts, such as causality, space, and time, and, above all, logic. We must also keep in mind that these phenomena are genuine and spontaneous expressions of human personality, each incident unique unto itself. For that reason alone there is little hope of ever reproducing true ESP phenomena in a laboratory or squeezing the occurrences into the narrow confines of statistics. Only by the competent observation of a large body of such phenomena and the deduction of reasonable conclusions therefrom can we hope to learn how ESP phenomena work and when.

This book is not primarily a case book, giving examples of the literally hundreds of thousands of authenticated cases of ESP throughout the world. There will be some outstanding examples of ESP, but they will be quoted here merely in the context of proof that the phenomena are common and plentiful. My prime purpose in writing this work is to help students and laymen alike understand the nature of ESP and how it works. My views are my own, but they are based upon twenty years of intensive study and large numbers of cases from my personal files and recollection. Since it is my conviction that ESP phenomena are possible to all of us, excluding only those who are obviously incapacitated in mind and body, I wish to help people develop their incipient ESP capabilities from the beginning, when they first notice their talents in this area. Just like any other human faculty, ESP can be enhanced and enlarged by certain techniques, practices, attitudes, and other forms of relationship between subject and capability. The techniques worked out for this book are my personal convictions and do not necessarily represent the opinion of the entire field or other parapsychologists, but I have found them to be useful and productive of results in my years of work with subjects, whether they be laymen or students at the college where I teach parapsychology, the New York Institute of Technology.

Lastly, the development of ESP in man is by no means a substitute for other talents or an alternate way of finding fulfillment. Whatever one's aim in life is, however, the mastering of ESP can be most helpful in bringing it about.

THE TRUTH ABOUT ESP

CHAPTER I

SCIENCE AND ESP

Sometimes a well-meaning but otherwise unfamiliar reporter will ask me, "How does science feel about ESP?" That is a little like asking how mathematics teachers feel about Albert Einstein. ESP is part of science. Some scientists in other areas may have doubts about its validity or its potentials, just as scientists in one area frequently doubt scientists in other areas. For example, some chemists doubt what some medical men say about the efficiency of certain drugs, or some underwater explorers differ with the opinions expressed by space explorers, and some medical doctors differ greatly with what other medical doctors believe. A definition of science is in order. Contrary to what some people think, science is not knowledge or even comparable to the idea of knowledge; science is merely the process of gathering knowledge by reliable and recognized means. These means, however, may change as time goes on, and the means considered reliable in the past may fail the test in the future, while, conversely, new methods not used in the past may come into prominence and be found useful. To consider the edifice of science an immovable object, a wall against which one may safely lean with confidence in the knowledge that nearly everything worth knowing is already known, is a most unrealistic concept. Just as a living thing changes from day to day, so does science and that which makes up scientific evidence.

There are, however, forces within science representing the conservative or establishment point of view. These forces are vested in certain powerful individuals who are not so much unconvinced of the reality of controversial phenomena and the advisability of including these phe- nomena in the scientific process as they are unwilling to change their established concept of science. They are, in short, unwilling to learn new and startling facts, many of which are in conflict with that which they have learned in the past, that which forms the very basis and foundation of their scientific beliefs. Science derives from *scire,* mean- ing to know. *Scientia,* the Latin noun upon which our English term science is based, is best translated as "the ability to know," or perhaps as "understanding." Knowl- edge as an absolute is another matter. I doubt very much that absolute knowledge is possible even within the con- fines of human comprehension. What we are dealing with in science is a method of reaching out toward it, not at- taining it. In the end, the veil of secrecy will hide the ultimate truth from us, very likely because we are in- capable of grasping it due to insufficient spiritual aware- ness. This insufficiency expresses itself, among other ways, in a determined reliance upon terminology and frames of reference derived from materialistic concepts that have little bearing upon the higher strata of information. Every form of research requires its own set of tools and its own criteria. To apply the purely materialistic empiric con- cepts of evidence to nonmaterialistic areas is not likely to yield satisfactory results. An entirely different set of criteria must be established first before we can hope to grasp the significance of those nonmaterial concepts and forces around us which have been with us since the beginning of time, which are both within us and without us and which form the innermost layer of human consciousness as well as the outer reaches of the existing universe.

By and large, the average scientist not directly concerned with the field of ESP and parapsychology does not venture into it, either pro or con. He is usually too much concerned with his own field and with the insufficiencies found in his own bailiwick. Occasionally, people in areas that are peripheral to ESP and parapsychology will venture into it, partly because they are attracted by it and sense a growing importance in the study of those areas that have so long been neglected by most scientists, partly because they feel that in attacking the findings of parapsychology they are in some psychologically understandable way validating their own failures. When Professor Joseph B. Rhine first started out at Duke University to measure what he called the "PSI" force in man, critics were quick to point out the hazards of a system relying so heavily on contrived, artificial conditions and statistics. Whatever Professor Rhine was able to prove in the way of significant data has since been largely obscured by criticism, some of it valid and some of it not, and of course by the far greater importance of observing spontaneous phenomena in the field when and if they occur. At the beginning, however, Professor Rhine at his laboratory at Duke University represented a milestone in scientific thinking. It was the first time that

the area formerly completely left to the occultist was being explored by a trained scientist in the modern sense of
the term. Even then no one took the field of parapsychology very seriously; Rhine and his closest associate, Dr.
Hornell Hart, were considered part of the Department of
Sociology as there had not as yet been a distinct Department of Parapsychology or a degree in that new
science. Even today there is no doctorate in it and those
working in the field usually have to have other credits as
well. But the picture is changing. A few years ago, Dr.
Jules Eisenbud of the University of Colorado, Denver,
startled the world with his disclosures of the peculiar
talents of a certain Ted Serios, a Chicago bellhop gifted
with psychic photography talents. This man could project
images into a camera or television tube, some of which
were from the so-called future while others were from
distant places Mr. Serios had never been to. The experiments were undertaken under the most rigid test conditions; they were repeated, something the old-line scientists
in parapsychology stressed over and over again. Despite
the abundant amount of evidence, produced in the glaring
limelight of public attention and under strictest scientific
test conditions, some of Dr. Eisenbud's colleagues at the
University of Colorado turned away from him whenever
he asked them to witness the experiments he was then
conducting. So great was the prejudice against anything
Eisenbud and his associates might find in contravention
of existing concepts that men of science couldn't bear to
find out for themselves, afraid to unlearn a great deal.
Today, even orthodox scientists are willing to listen a
little more; still, it is a far cry from having an actual in-

stitute of paraspsychology independent of existent facil-
ities, which I have been advocating for many years. But
there is a greater willingness to evaluate the evidence
fairly and without prejudice on the part of those who
represent the bulk of the scientific establishment.

Most big corporate decisions are made illogically, according to John Mihalasky, associate professor of management engineering at the Newark College of Engineering.
The professor contends that logical people can understand a scientific explanation of an illogical process. "Experiments conducted by Professor Mihalasky demonstrate
a correlation between superior management ability and
an executive's extrasensory perception or ESP." According
to the New York *Times* of August 31, 1969, "research in
ESP had been conducted at the college since 1962 to determine if there was a correlation between managerial
talent and ESP. There are tests in extrasensory perception
and also in precognition, the ability to foretell events before they happen. The same precognition tests may also
be of use in selecting a person of superior creative ability."
But the business side of the research establishment was
by no means alone in taking slow cognizance of the validity and value of ESP. According to an interview in the
Los Angeles *Times* of August 30, 1970, psychiatrist Dr.
George Sjolund of Baltimore, Maryland, has concluded,
"All the evidence does indicate that ESP exists." Dr.
Sjolund works with people suspected of having ESP
talents and puts them through various tests in specially
built laboratories. Scientific experiments designed to test
for the existence of ESP are rare. Dr. Sjolund knows of

only one other like it in the United States—in Seattle. Sjolund does ESP work only one day a week. His main job is acting director of research at Spring Grove State Hospital.

According to Evelyn de Wolfe, Los Angeles *Times* staff writer, "The phenomenon of ESP remains inconclusive, ephemeral and mystifying but for the first time in the realm of science, no one is ashamed to say they believe there is such a thing." The writer quotes this observation by Dr. Thelma S. Moss, assistant professor of medical pychology at UCLA School of Medicine, who has been conducting experiments in parapsychology for several years. In a report dated June 12, 1969, the science writer also says, "In a weekend symposium on ESP more than six hundred persons in the audience learned that science is dealing seriously with the subject of haunted houses, clairvoyance, telepathy, and psychokinesis and is attempting to harness the unconscious mind."

It is not surprising that some more liberally inclined and enlightened scientists are coming around to thinking that there is something in ESP after all. Back in 1957, *Life* magazine editorialized on "A Crisis in Science": "New enigmas in physics revive quests in metaphysics. From the present chaos of science's conceptual universe two facts might strike the layman as significant. One is that the old-fashioned materialism is now even more old-fashioned. Its basic assumption—that the only 'reality' is that which occupies space and has a mass—is irrelevant to an age that has proved that matter is interchangeable

with energy. Second conclusion is that old-fashioned
metaphysics, so far from being irrelevant to an age of
science, is science's indispensable complement for a full
view of life. Physicists acknowledge as much; a current
Martin advertisement says that their rocket men's shop-
talk includes 'the physics (and metaphysics) of their
work. Metaphysical speculation is becoming fashionable
again. Set free of materialism, metaphysics could well become man's chief preoccupation of the next century and
may even yield a world-wide consensus on the nature of
life and the universe.'"

By 1971, this prophetic view of *Life* magazine took on
new dimensions of reality. According to the Los Angeles
Times of February 11, 1971, Apollo 14 astronaut Edgar D.
Mitchell attempted to send mental messages to a Chicago
engineer whose hobby is extrasensory perception. Using
ESP cards, which he had taken aboard with him to
transfer messages to Chicago psychic Olaf Olsen, Mitchell
managed to prove beyond any doubt that telepathy works
even from the outer reaches of space. The Mitchell–
Olsen experiment has since become part of the history of
parapsychology. Not only did it add significantly to the
knowledge of how telepathy really works, it made a
change in the life of the astronaut, Mitchell. According
to an UPI dispatch dated September 27, 1971, Mitchell
became convinced that life existed away from earth and
more than likely in our own galaxy. But he doubted that
physical space travel held all the answers. "If the phenomenon of astral projection has any validity, it might be
perfectly valid to use it in intergalactic travel"; Mitchell

indicated that he was paying additional attention to ESP for future use. Since that time, of course, Mr. Mitchell has become an active experimenter in ESP.

A few years ago I appeared at the University of Bridgeport (Connecticut) lecturing on scientific evidence for the existence of ghosts. My lecture included some slides taken under test conditions and attracted some 1,200 students and faculty members. As a result of this particular demonstration, I met Robert Jeffries, professor of mechanical engineering at the university and an avid parapsychologist. During the years of our friendship Professor Jeffries and I tried very hard to set up an independent institute of parapsychology. We had thought that Bob Jeffries, also at one time president of his own data-processing company, would be particularly acceptable to the business community. But the executives he saw were not the least bit interested in giving any money to such a project. They failed to see the practical implications of studying ESP. Perhaps they were merely not in tune with the trend, even among the business executives.

In an article dated October 23, 1969, *The Wall Street Journal* headline was "Strange Doings. Americans Show Burst of Interest in Witches, Other Occult Matters." The piece, purporting to be a survey of the occult scene and written by Stephen J. Sansweet, presents the usual hodgepodge of information and misinformation, lumping witches and werewolves together with parapsychologists and researchers. He quotes Mortimer R. Feinberg, a psychology professor at City University of New York, as saying, "The closer we get to a controlled, totally predictable society, the more man becomes fearful of the consequences." Sansweet then goes on to say that occult supplies, books, and even such peripheral things as jewelry are being gobbled up by an interested public, a sure sign that the occult is "in." Although the "survey" is on the level of a Sunday supplement piece and really quite worthless, it does indicate the seriousness with which the business community regards the occult field, appearing, as it did, on the front page of *The Wall Street Journal.*

More realistic and respectable is an article in the magazine *Nation's Business* of April 1971 entitled "Dollars May Flow from the Sixth Sense. Is there a link between business success and extrasensory perception?" "We think the role of precognition deserves special consideration in sales forecasting. Wittingly or unwittingly, it is probably already used there. Much more research needs to be done on the presence and use of precognition among executives but the evidence we have obtained indicates that such research will be well worthwhile."

As far back as 1955 the Anderson Laboratories of Brookline, Massachusetts, were in the business of forecasting the future. Its president, Frank Anderson, stated, "Anderson Laboratories is in a position to furnish weekly charts showing what, in all probability, the stock market will do in each coming week." Anderson's concept, or, as he calls it, the Anderson Law, involves predictions based upon the study of many things, from the moon tides to human behavior to elements of parapsychology. He had done this type of work for at least twenty-five years prior to setting up the laboratories. Most of his predictions are based upon calculated trends and deal in finances and politics. Anderson claimed that his accuracy rate was 86 per cent accurate with airplane accidents because they come in cycles, 92.6 per cent accurate in the case of major fires, 84 per cent accurate with automobile accidents, and that his evaluations could be used for many business purposes, from advertising campaigns to executive changes to new product launchings and even to the planning of entertainment; in politics, Anderson proposes to help chart, ahead of time, the possible outcome of political campaigns. He even deals with hunting and fishing forecasts, and since the latter two occupations are particularly dear to the heart of the business community, it would appear that Anderson has it wrapped up in one neat little package.

Professor R. A. McConnell, Department of Biophysics and Microbiology, University of Pittsburgh, Pennsylvania, wrote in an article published by the *American Psychologist* in May 1968 that in discussing ESP before psychology students, it was not unusual to speak of the credulity of the public, while he felt it more necessary to examine instead the credibility of scientists, including both those for ESP and those against it. Referring to an article on ESP by the British researcher G. R. Price published by *Science* in 1955, Professor McConnell pointed to Price's contention that proof of ESP was conclusive only if one were to accept the good faith and sanity of the experimenters, but that it could easily be explained away if one were to assume that the experimenters, working in collaboration with their witnesses, had intentionally faked the results. McConnell went on to point out that this unsubstantiated suggestion of fraud by Price, a chemist by profession, was being published on the first page of the most influential scientific journal in America.

A lot of time has passed since 1955: the American Association for the Advancement of Science has recently voted the Parapsychology Association into membership. The latter, one of several bodies of scientific investigators in the field of parapsychology, had sought entrance into the association for many years but had been barred from membership by the alleged prejudices of those in control of the association. The Parapsychology Association itself, due to a fine irony, had also barred some reputable researchers from membership in its own ranks for the very same reasons. Once the dam burst, parapsychology became an accepted subject within the American Association for the Advancement of Science. Doing research in a reputable fashion in the field, they were invited to join. My own New York Committee for the Investigation of Paranormal Occurrences, founded in 1962 under the sponsorship of Eileen Garrett, president of the Parapsychology Foundation, Inc., is also a member of the American Association for the Advancement of Science.

Professor McConnell pointed out the fallibility of certain textbooks considered bulwarks of scientific knowledge. He reminded his audience that until the year 1800 the highest scientific authorities thought that there were no such things as meteorites until the leaders of science found out that meteorites come from outer space, and the textbooks were rewritten accordingly. What disturbed Professor McConnell was that the revised textbooks did not mention that there had been an argument about the matter. He wonders how many arguments are still going on in science and how many serious mistakes are in the textbooks we use for study. In his opinion, we ought to believe only one half of the ideas expressed in the works on biological sciences, although he is not sure *which* half. In his view, ESP belongs in psychology, one of the biological sciences, and he feels that ESP is something about which so-called authorities are in error. McConnell pointed out that most psychology textbooks omit the subject entirely as unworthy of serious consideration. But in his opinion, the books are wrong, for ESP is a real psychological phenomenon. He also showed that the majority of those doing serious research in ESP are not psychologists, and deduces from this and the usual textbook treatment of the subject as well as from his own sources that psychologists are simply not interested in ESP.

L. C. Kling, M.D., is a psychiatrist living in Strasbourg, France. He writes in German and has published occasional papers dealing with his profession. Most psychiatrists and pychoanalysts who base their work upon the findings of Sigmund Freud, as well they should, balk at the idea that Dr. Freud had any interest in psychic phenomena or ESP. But the fact is—and Dr. Kling points this out in an article published in 1966—that Freud had many encounters with paranormal phenomena. When he was sixty-five years old he wrote to American researcher Herewood Carrington, "If I had to start my life over again I would rather be a parapsychologist than a psychoanalyst." And toward the end of his life he confessed to his biographer E. Jones that he would not hesitate to bring upon himself the hostility of the professional world in order to champion an unpopular point of view. What made him say this was a particularly convincing case of telepathy that he had come across.

In June of 1966 the German physicist Dr. Werner Schiebeler gave a lecture concerning his findings on the subject of physical research methods applicable to parapsychology. The occasion was the conference on parapsychology held at the city of Constance in Germany. Dr. Schiebeler, as well versed in atom physics as he is in parapsychology, suggested that memory banks from deceased entities could be established independent of physical brain matter. "If during séances entities, phantoms, or spirits of the deceased appear which have been identified beyond a shadow of a doubt to be the people they pretend to be, they must be regarded as something more than images of the dead. Otherwise we would have to consider people in the physical life whom we have not seen for some time and encounter again today as merely copies of a former existence." Dr. Schiebeler goes on to say that in his opinion parapsychology has furnished definite proof for the continuance of life beyond physical death.

This detailed and very important paper was presented in written form to the eminent German parapsychologist Dr. Hans Bender, head of the Institute of Borderline Sciences at the University of Freiburg, Germany. Since it contained strong evidence of a survivalist nature, and since Dr. Bender has declared himself categorically opposed to the concept of personal survival after death, the paper remains unanswered, and Dr. Schiebeler was unable to get any response from the institute.

Despite the fact that several leading universities are doing around-the-clock research in ESP, there are still those who wish it weren't so. Dr. Walter Alvarez writes in the Los Angeles *Times* of January 23, 1972, "In a recent issue of the medical journal *M.D.*, there was an interesting article on a subject which interests many physicians and patients. Do mediums really make contact with a dead person at a séance?" He then goes on to quote an accusation of fraudulence against the famous Fox sisters, who first brought spirit rappings to public attention in 1848. "Curiously, a number of very able persons have accepted the reality of spiritualism and some have been very much interested in what goes on in séances," Dr. Alvarez reports. Carefully, he points out the few and better-known cases of alleged fraud among world-famous mediums such as Eusepia Palladino, omitting the fact that the Italian medium had been highly authentic to the very end and that fakery had never been conclusively proven in her case. There isn't a single word about Professor Rhine or any research in the field of parapsychology in this article.

Perhaps not on the same level, but certainly with even greater popular appeal, is a "Dear Abbey" reply printed by the same Los Angeles *Times* on November 5, 1969, concerning an inquiry from a reader on how to find a reputable medium because she wanted to get in touch with her dead husband. To this "Dear Abbey" replied,

"Many have claimed they can communicate with the dead, but so far no one has been able to prove it."

Perhaps one can forgive such uninformed people as those just quoted their negative attitude toward psychic phenomena if one looks at some of the less desirable practices lately multiplying in the field. Take, for instance, the publisher of *Penthouse* magazine, an English competitor to our own native *Playboy*. A prize of £25,000 was to be paid to anyone producing paranormal phenomena under test conditions. A panel consisting of Sir George Joy, Society for Psychical Research, Professor H. H. Price, Canon John Pearce-Higgins, and leading psychical researcher Mrs. Kathleen Goldney resigned in protest when they took a good look at the pages of the magazine and discovered that it was more concerned with bodies than with spirits.

The *Psychic Register International*, of Phoenix, Arizona, proclaims its willingness to list everyone in the field so that they may present to the world a *Who's Who in the Psychic World*. A parapsychology guidance institute in St. Petersburg, Florida, advised me that they are preparing a bibliography of technical books in the field of parapsychology. The Institute of Psychic Studies of Parkersburg, West Virginia, claimed that "for the first time in the United States a college of psychic studies entirely dedicated to parapsychology offering a two-year course leading to a doctorate in psychic sciences is being opened and will be centrally located in West Virginia." The list of courses of study sounded very impressive and included three credits for the mind (study of the brain), background of parapsychology (three credits), and such fascinating things as magic in speech (three credits), explaining superstitions attributed to magic; students will be taught secrets of prestidigitation. The list of courses was heavily studded with grammatical errors and misspellings. Psychic Dimensions Incorporated of New York City, according to an article in the New York *Times*, no less, of December 4, 1970, "has got it all together," the "all" meaning individual astrologists, graphologists, as well as occasional palmists, psychometrists, or those astute in the reading of tarot cards. According to the writer of the article, Lisa Hammel, the founder of the booking agency, William J. Danielle, has "about 150 metaphysical personalities under his wing and is ready to book for a variety of occasions." The master of this enterprise is quoted as explaining, "I had to create an entertainment situation because people will not listen to facts." Mr. Danielle originally started with a memorable event called "Breakfast with a Witch" starring none other than Witch Hazel, a pretty young waitress from New Jersey who has established her claim to witchcraft on various public occasions.

"Six leading authorities on mental telepathy, psychic experiences and metaphysics will conduct a panel discussion on extrasensory perception, said the New York *Daily News* of January 24, 1971. The meeting was being held under the auspices of the Society for the Study of Parapsychology and Metaphysics. As if that name were not impressive enough, there is even a subdivision entitled the National Committee for the Study of Metaphysical Sciences. But it turned out that the experts were indeed authorities in their respective fields. They included Dr.

Gertrude Schmeidler of City College, New York, and well-known psychic Ron Warmoth. A colleague of mine, Raymond Van Over of Hofstra University, was also aboard. Although I heard nothing further of the Society for the Study of Parapsychology and Metaphysics, it seemed like a reputable organization, or rather attempt at an organization. Until then about the only reputable organization known to most individuals interested in the study of ESP was, and is, of course, the American Society for Psychical Research located at 5 West Seventy-third Street in New York City. But the society, originally founded by Dr. J. Hislop, has become rather conservative. It rarely publishes any controversial findings any more. Its magazine is extremely technical and likely to discourage the beginning student. Fortunately, however, it also publishes the ASPR *Newsletter*, which is somewhat more democratic and popularly styled. The society still ignores parapsychologists who do not conform to their standards, especially people like myself, who frequently appear on television and make definite statements on psychic matters that the society would rather leave in balance. Many of the legacies that help support the American Society for Psychical Research were given in the hope that the society might establish some definite proof for survival of human personality after death and for answers to other important scientific questions. If researchers such as I proclaim such matters to be already proven, there would seem to be little left for the society to prove in the future. But individual leaders of the society are more outspoken in their views. Dr. Gardner Murphy, long-time president of the society and formerly connected with the Menninger Foundation, observed, "If there was one tenth of the evidence in any other field of science than there is in parapsychology, it would be accepted beyond question." Dr. Lawrence L. Le Shan, Ph.D., writer and investigator, says, "Parapsychology is far more than it appears to be on first glance. In the most profound sense it is the study of the basic nature of man." Dr. Le Shan goes on to say, "There is more to man, more to him and his relationship with the cosmos than we have accepted. Further, this 'more' is of a different kind and order from the parts we know about. We have the data and they are strong and clear but they could not exist if man were only what we have believed him to be. If he were only flesh and bone, if he worked on the same type of principles as a machine, if he were really as separated from other men as we have thought, it would be impossible for him to do the things we know he sometimes does. The 'impossible facts' of ESP tell us of a part of man long hidden in the mists of legend, art, dream, myth and mysticism, which our explorers of reality in the last ninety years have demonstrated to be scientifically valid, to be real."

While the bickering between those accepting the reality of ESP phenomena and those categorically rejecting them was still being conducted in the United States, the Russians came up with a startling coup: they went into the field wholesale and at this time there are at least eight major universities in the Soviet Union with full-time, full-staffed research centers in parapsychology. What is more, there are no restrictions placed upon those working in this field, and they are free to publish anything they like, whether or not it conforms to dialectic Marxism. This came as rather a shock to the American scientific establishment. In her review of the amazing book by Sheila Ostrander and Lynn Schroeder, *Psychic Discoveries Behind the Iron Curtain,* Dr. Thelma Moss of the University of California, Los Angeles School of Medicine, said, "If the validity of their statements is proved, then the American scientist is faced with the magnificent irony that in 1970 Soviet materialistic science has pulled off a coup in the field of occult phenomena equal to that of Sputnik rising into space in 1957."

From this work and other reports from Russia it would appear that the Russians are years ahead of us in applying techniques of ESP to practical usage. Allegedly, they have learned to use hypnosis at a distance, they have shown us photographs of experiments in psychokinesis, or the willful moving of objects by mental powers alone and even in Kirlian photography, showing the life-force fields around living things. Nat Freedland, reviewing the book for the Los Angeles *Times,* said, "Scientists in Eastern Europe have been succeeding with astonishingly far-reaching parapsychology experiments for years. The scope of what Communist countries like Russia, Czechoslovakia, and even little Bulgaria have accomplished in controlled scientific PSI experiments makes the Western brand of ESP look namby-pamby indeed. Instead of piddling around endlessly with decks of cards and dice like Dr. J. B. Rhine of Duke University, Soviet scientist put one telepathically talented experimenter in Moscow and another in Siberia twelve hundred miles away."

Shortly afterward, the newspapers were filled with articles dealing with the Russians and their telepaths or experimenters. Word had it that the Russians had a woman who was possessed of bioplasmic energy and who could move objects by mental concentration. This woman, Nina Kulagina, was photographed doing just that. William Rice, science writer for the *Daily News*, asked his readers, "Do you have ESP? It's hard to prove, but hard to deny." The piece itself is the usual hodgepodge of information and conjecture but it shows how far-reaching the interest in ESP has gone in the United States. Of course, the two young ladies who went behind the Iron Curtain to explore the realms of parapsychology did not exactly tread on virgin territory. Those active in the field of parapsychology in the United States had long been familiar with the work of Professor L. Vasiliev. The Russian scientist's books are standard fare on any bookshelf in this field. Dr. I. M. Kogan, chairman of the Investigation Commission of Russian Scientists dealing with ESP, is quoted as saying that he believes "many people have the ability to receive and transmit telepathic information, but the faculty is undeveloped."

And what was being done on the American side during the time the Russians were developing their parapsychology laboratories and teams of observers? Mae West gave a magnificent party at her palatial estate in Hollywood during which her favorite psychic, "Dr." Richard Ireland, the psychic from Phoenix, performed what the guests referred to as amazing feats. Make no mistake about it, Mae West is serious about her interest in parapsychology. She even lectured on the subject some time ago at a university. But predicting the future for invited guests and charming them at the same time is a far cry from setting up a sober institute for parapsychology where the subject can be dealt with objectively and around the clock.

On a more practical level, controversial Dutchman Peter Hurkos, who fell off a ladder and discovered his telepathic abilities some years back, was called in to help the police to find clues when the Tate murder was in the headlines. Hurkos did describe one of the raiders as bearded and felt that there were overtones of witchcraft in the assault. About that time, also, Bishop James Pike told the world in headline-making news conferences that he had spoken to his dead son through various mediums. "There is enough scientific evidence to give plausible affirmation that the human personality survives the grave. It is the most plausible explanation of the phenomena that occurred," Bishop Pike is quoted.

Over in Britain, Rosemary Brown was getting messages from dead composers, including such kingpins as Beethoven, Chopin, Schubert, and Debussy. Her symphonies, attributed to her ESP capabilities, have even been recorded. When I first heard about the amazing Miss Brown, I was inclined to dismiss the matter unless some private, as yet unpublished, information about the personal lives of the dead composers was also brought out by the medium. Apparently, this is what happened in the course of time and continued investigations. I have never met Miss Brown, but one of the investigators sent to Britain to look into the case was a man whom I knew well, Stewart Robb, who had the advantage of being both a parapsychologist and a music expert. It is his opinion that the Rosemary Brown phenomenon is indeed genuine, but Miss Brown is by no means the only musical medium. According to the *National Enquirer*, British medium Leslie Flint, together with two friends, Sydney Woods and Mrs. Betty Greene, claimed to have captured on tape the voices of more than two hundred famous personalities, including Frédéric Chopin and Oscar Wilde.

Gradually, however, the cleavage between the occult or mystically, emotionally tinged form of inquiry into psychic phenomena, and the purely scientific, clinically oriented way becomes more apparent. That is not to say that both methods will not eventually merge into one single quest for truth—far from it. Only by using all avenues of approach to a problem can we truly accomplish its solution, but it seems to me very necessary at this time when so many people are becoming acquainted with the occult, and parapsychology in general, to make a clear distinction between a tearoom reader and a professor of parapsychology, between a person who has studied psychical phenomena for twenty-five years and has all the necessary academic credits and a Johnny-come-lately who has crept out of the woodwork of opportunism to start his own "research" center or society. Those who sincerely seek information in this field should question the credentials of those who give them answers; well-known names are always preferable to names one has never heard before. Researchers with academic credentials or affiliations are more likely to be trusted than those who offer merely paper doctorates fresh from the printing press. Lastly, psychic readers purporting to be great prophets must be examined at face value—on the basis of their accomplishments in each individual case, not upon their self-proclaimed reputation. With all that in mind and with due caution, it is still heartwarming to find so many sincere and serious people dedicating themselves more and more to the field of parapsychology and scientific inquiry into what seems to me one of the most fascinating areas of human endeavor. Ever since the late Sir Oliver Lodge proclaimed, "Psychic research is the most important field in the world today, by far the most important," I have felt quite the same way.

At Washington University, St. Louis, Missouri, a dedicated group of researchers with no funds to speak of has been trying to delve into the mystery of psychic photography. Following in the footsteps of Dr. Jules Eisenbud of the University of Colorado, and my own work *Psychic Photography—Threshold of a New Science?* this group, under the aegis of the Department of Physics at the university, is attempting to "produce psychic photographs with some regularity under many kinds of situations." The group feels that since Ted Serios discovered his ability in this field by accident, others might have similar abilities. "Only when we have found a good subject can the real work of investigating the nature of psychic photography begin," they explain. The fact that people associated with a department of physics at a major American university even speak of investigating psychic photography scientifically is so much of a novelty, considering the slurs heaped upon this subject for so many years by the majority of establishment scientists, that one can only hope that a new age in unbiased science is indeed dawning upon us.

Stanley Korn of Maryland has a degree in physics and has done graduate work in mathematics, statistics, and psychology; he is currently employed by the Navy as an operations research analyst. Through newspaper advertisements he discovered the Silva Mind Control Course and took it, becoming acquainted with Silva's approach, including the awareness of the alpha state of brain-wave activity, which is associated with increased problem-solving ability and, of course, ESP. "What induced me to take the course was the rather astonishing claim made by the lecturer that everyone taking the course would be able to function psychically to his own satisfaction or get his money back. This I had to see," Mr. Korn explained. Describing the Silva Method, which incorporates some of the elements of diagnosis developed by the late Edgar Cayce but combines it with newer techniques and what, for want of a better term, we call traveling clairvoyance, Mr. Korn learned that psychic activities are not necessarily limited to diagnosing health cases, but can also be employed in psychometry, the location of missing objects and persons, and even the locations of malfunctions in automobiles. "After seeing convincing evidence for the existence of PSI, and experiencing the phenomenon myself, I naturally wanted to know the underlying principles governing its operation. To date, I have been unable to account for the psychic transmission of information by any of the known forms of energy, such as radio waves. The phenomena can be demonstrated at will, making controlled experiments feasible."

But the mind-control approach is by no means the only new thing in the search for awareness and full use of ESP powers in man. People working in the field of physics are used to apparatus, to test equipment, to physical tools. Some of these people have become interested in the marginal areas of parapsychology and ESP research, hoping to contribute some new mechanical gadget to the field. According to the magazine *Purchasing Week,* new devices utilizing infrared light to pinpoint the location of an otherwise unseen intruder by the heat radiating from his body have been developed. *Time* magazine of August 17, 1970, headlines in its science section, "Thermography: Coloring with Heat." The magazine explained that "infrared detectors are providing stunning images that were once totally invisible to the naked eye. The new medium is called color thermography, the technique of translating heat rays into color. Unlike ordinary color photographs, which depend on reflected visible light, thermograms or heat pictures respond only to the temperature of the subject. Thus the thermographic camera can work with equal facility in the dark or light. The camera's extraordinary capability is built around a characteristic of all objects, living or inanimate. Because their atoms are constantly in motion, they give off some degree of heat or infrared radiation. If the temperature rises high enough, the radiation may become visible to the human eye, as in the red glow of a blast furnace. Ordinarily, the heat emissions remain locked in the invisible range of infrared light."

It is clear that such equipment can be of great help in examining so-called haunted houses, psychically active areas, or psychometric objects; in other words, to step in where the naked eye cannot help, or where ordinary photography discloses nothing unusual. The magazine *Electronics World* of April 1970, in an article entitled "Electronics and Parapsychology" by L. George Lawrence, says, "One of the most intriguing things to emerge in that area is the now famous *Backster Effect.* Since living plants seem to react bioelectrically to thought images directed to their over-all well-being, New Jersey cytologist Dr. H. Miller thinks that the phenomenon is based upon a type of cellular consciousness. These and related considerations lead to the idea that PSI is but a part of a so-called paranormal matrix—a unique communications grid that binds all life together. Its phenomena apparently work on a multi-input basis which operates beyond the known physical laws."

Lanston Monotype Company of Philadelphia, Pennsylvania, manufactures photomechanical apparatus and has done some work in the ESP field. The company is trying to develop testing equipment of use to parapsychologists. Superior Vending Company of Brockton, Massachusetts, through its design engineer, R. K. Golka, offered me a look into the matter of a newly developed image intensifier tube developed by research for possible use in a portable television camera capable of picking up the fine imprints left behind in the atmosphere of haunted areas. "The basic function of this tube is to intensify and pick up weak images picked up by the television camera. These are images which would otherwise not be seen or go unnoticed," the engineer explained. Two years later, Mr. Golka, who had by then set up his own company of electronic consultants, suggested experiments with spontaneous ionization. "If energy put into the atmosphere could be coupled properly with the surrounding medium, air, then huge amounts of ionization could result. If there were a combination of frequency and wave length that would remove many of the electron shells of the common elements of our atmosphere, that too would be of great scientific value. Of course, the electrons would fall back at random so there would be shells producing white light or fluorescence. This may be similar to the flashes of light seen by people in a so-called haunted house. In any event, if this could be done by the output of very small energies such as those coming from the human brain of microvolt and micro amp range, it would be quite significant." Mr. Golka responded to my suggestion that ionization of the air accompanied many of the psychic phenomena where visual manifestations had been observed. I have held that a change occurs in the atmosphere when psychic energies are present, and that the change includes ionization of the surrounding air or ether. "Some of the things you have mentioned over the years seem to fit into this puzzle. I don't know if science has all the pieces yet but I feel we have a good handful to work with," Mr. Golka concluded in his suggestions to me. Since that time some progress has been made in the exploration of perception by plants, and the influence of human emotions on the growth of plants. Those seeking scientific data on these experiments may wish to examine Cleve Backster's report on "Evidence of a Primary Perception in Plant Life" in the *International Journal of Parapsychology*, Volume X, 1968. Backster maintains a research foundation at 165 West Forty-sixth Street in New York City.

Dr. Harry E. Stockman is head of Sercolab in Arlington, Massachusetts, specializing in apparatus in the fields of physics, electronics, and the medical profession. The company issues regular catalogues of their various devices, which range from simple classroom equipment to highly sophisticated research apparatus. The company, located at P. O. Box 78, Arlington, Massachusetts, has been in business for over twenty years. "In the case of mind-

over-matter parapsychology PK apparatus, our guarantee
applies only in the meaning that the apparatus will operate as stated in the hands of an accomplished sensitive.
Sercolab would not gamble its scientific reputation for the
good reason that mind-over-matter is a proven scientific
fact. It is so today thanks to the amazing breakthrough by
Georgia State University; this breakthrough does not
merely consist of the stunning performance of some students to be able to move a magnetic needle at a distance.
The breakthrough is far greater than that. It consists of
Georgia State University having devised a systematic
teaching technique, enabling some students in the class
to operate a magnetic needle by psychokinesis force,"
states the prospectus of the laboratory.

Obviously, science and ESP are merely casual acquaint-
ances at the present time. Many members of the family
are still looking askance at the new member of the community and wish it would simply go away and not bother
them. But parapsychology, the study of ESP, is here to
stay, like it or not. ESP research may be contrary to many
established scientific laws and its methodology differs
greatly from established practices. But it is a valid force;
it exists in every sense of the term; and it must be studied
fully in order to make an honest woman out of science in
the coming age. Anything less than that will lead scientific inquiry back to medieval thinking, back into the
narrow channels of prejudice and severely limited fields
of study. In the future, only a thorough re-examination of
the scientific position on ESP in general will yield greater
knowledge on the subject.

CHAPTER II

WHAT SORT OF PEOPLE ARE INTERESTED IN ESP?

The notion still persists among large segments of the population that ESP is a subject suitable only for very special people: the weird fringe, some far-out scientists perhaps, or those among the young people who are "into" the occult. Under no circumstances is it something respectable average citizens get involved with. An interest in ESP simply does not stand up alongside such interests as music, sports, or the arts. Anyone professing an interest in ESP is automatically classified as an oddball. This attitude is more pronounced in small towns than it is in sophisticated cities like New York, but until recently, at least, the notion that ESP can be a subject for average people on a broad basis was alien to the public mind. During the last few years, however, this attitude has shifted remarkably. More and more, people discussing the subject of extrasensory perception are welcomed in social circles as being unusual people, and become centers of attraction. Especially among the young, bringing up the subject of ESP almost guarantees one immediate friends. True, eyebrows are still raised among older people, especially business people or those in government, when ESP is raised as a serious subject matter. Occasionally one still hears the comment "You don't really believe in that stuff?" Occasionally, too, people will give you an argument trying to prove that it is all a fraud and has "long been proved to be without substance." It is remarkable how some of those avid scoffers quote "authoritative" sources, which they never identify by name or place. Even Professor Rhine is frequently being pictured as a man who tried to prove the reality of ESP but failed miserably.

Of course, we must realize that people believe that which they want to believe. If a concept becomes uncomfortable to a person, reasons for disbelief will be found even if they are sometimes dragged in out of left field. A well-known way of dismissing evidence for ESP is to quote only sources that are negative toward it. Several authors who thrive on "debunking books," undoubtedly the result of the current popularity of the occult subjects, make it their business to select a bibliography of source material that contains only the sort of proof they want in the light of their own prejudiced purpose. A balanced bibliography would, of course, yield different results and would thwart their efforts to debunk the subject of ESP. Sometimes people in official positions will deny the existence of factual material in order not to be confronted with the evidence, if that evidence tends to create a public image different from the one they wish to project.

A good case in point is an incident that occurred on the Chicago television broadcast emceed by columnist Irving Kupcinet. Among the guests appearing with me was Colonel "Shorty" Powers of NASA. I had just remarked that tests had been conducted among astronauts to determine whether they were capable of telepathy once the reaches of outer space had been entered, in case radio communications should prove to be inadequate. Colonel Powers rose indignantly, denouncing my statement as false, saying, in effect, that no tests had been undertaken among astronauts and that such a program lacked a basis of fact. Fortunately, however, I had upon me a letter on official NASA stationery, signed by Dr. M. Koneci, who was at the time head of that very project.

The types of people who are interested in ESP include some very strange bedfellows: on the one hand, there are increasing numbers of scientists delving into the area with newly designed tools and new methods; on the other hand, there are laymen in various fields who find ESP a fascinating subject and do not hesitate to admit their interest, nor do they disguise their belief that it works. Scientists have had to swallow their pride and discard many cherished theories about life. Those who were able to do so and adjust to the ever-changing pattern of what constitutes scientific proof found their studies in ESP most rewarding. The late heart specialist Dr. Alexis Carrel became interested in psychic phenomena, according to Monroe Fry in an article on ESP that recently appeared in *Esquire* magazine, during his famous experiment that established the immortality of individual cells in a fragment of chicken heart. "After he had been working on the problem for years somebody asked him about his conclusions. 'The work of a scientist is to observe facts,' he said, 'what I have observed are facts troublesome to science. But they are facts.' Science still knows very little about the human mind, but researchers are now certain that the mind is much more powerful and complicated than they have ever thought it was."

People accept theories, philosophies, or beliefs largely on the basis of who supports them, not necessarily on the facts alone. If a highly regarded individual supports a new belief, people are likely to follow him. Thus it was something of a shock to learn, several years after his passing, that Franklin Delano Roosevelt had frequently sat in séances during which his late mother, Sarah Delano, had appeared to him and given him advice in matters of state. It has quite definitely been established that King George V of England also attended séances. To this day, the English royal family is partial to psychical research although very little of this is ever published. Less secret is the case of Canada's late Prime Minister William Mac-kenzie King. According to *Life* magazine, which devoted several pages to King, he "was an ardent spiritualist who used mediums, the ouija board and a crystal ball for guidance in his private life." It is debatable whether this marks King a spiritualist or whether he was merely exercising his natural gift of ESP with an interest in psychical research.

I myself receive continual testimony that ESP is a fascinating subject to people who would not have thought of it a few years ago. Carlton R. Adams, Rear Admiral, U. S. Navy retired, having read one of my books, contacted me to discuss my views on reincarnation. John D. Grayson, associate professor of linguistics at Sir George Williams

University, Montreal, Canada, said, "If I lived in New York, I should like nothing better than to enroll in your eight-lecture course on parapsychology." Gerald S. O'Morrow has a doctorate in education and is at Indiana State University: "I belong to a small development group which meets weekly and has been doing such for the last two years." A lady initialed S.D. writes from California, "I have been successful in working a ouija board for eight years on a serious basis and have tried automatic writing with a small but significant amount of success. I have a great desire to develop my latent powers but until now I haven't known who to go to that I could trust." The lady's profession is that of a police matron with a local police department.

A.P. gives a remarkable account of ESP experiences over the past twenty years. His talents include both visual and auditory phenomena. In reporting his incidents to me, he asked for an appraisal of his abilities with ESP. By profession A.P. is a physician, a native of Cuba.

S. B. Barris contacted me for an appraisal of his ESP development in the light of a number of incidents in which he found himself capable of foretelling the result of a race, whether or not a customer would conclude the sale he was hoping for and several incidents of clairvoyance. Mr. Barris, in addition to being a salesman in mutual funds, is an active member of the United States Army Reserves with the rank of major.

Stanley R. Dean, M.D., clinical professor of psychiatry at the University of Florida, is a member of the American Psychiatric Association Task Force on transcultural psychiatry and the recent co-ordinator of a symposium at which a number of parapsychologists spoke.

Curiously enough, the number of people who will accept the existence of ESP is much larger than the number of people who believe in spirit survival or the more advanced forms of occult beliefs. ESP has the aura of the scientific about it, while, to the average mind at least, subjects including spirit survival, ghosts, reincarnation, and such require seemingly other facets of human acceptance than the purely scientific. That, at least, is a widely held conviction. At the basis of this distinction lies the unquestionable fact that there is a very pronounced difference between ESP and the more advanced forms of occult scientific belief. For ESP to work one need not accept survival of human personality beyond bodily death. ESP between the living is as valid as ESP between the living and the so-called dead. Telepathy works whether one partner is in the great beyond or not. In fact, a large segment of the reported phenomena involving clairvoyance can probably be explained on the basis of simple ESP and need not involve the intercession of spirits at all. It has always been a debatable issue whether a medium obtains information about a client from a spirit source standing by, as it were, in the wings, or whether the medium obtains this information from his own unconscious mind, drawing upon extraordinary powers dormant within it. Since the results are the main concern of the client, it is generally of little importance whence the information originates. It is, of course, comforting to think that ESP is merely an extension of the ordinary five senses as we know them, and can be accepted without the need for overhauling one's philosophy. The same cannot be said about the acceptance of spirit communication, reincarnation, and other occult phenomena. Accepting them as realities requires a profound alteration in the ordinary philosophy, at least among average people. With ESP, a scientifically oriented person need only extend the limits of believability a little, comparing the ESP faculty to radio waves and himself to a receiving instrument.

So widespread is the interest in ESP research and so many are the published cases indicating its reality that the number of out-and-out debunkers has shrunk considerably during the past years. Some years ago a chemist named H. H. Pierce seriously challenged the findings of Dr. Joseph Rhine on the grounds that his statistics were false, if not fraudulent, and that the material proved nothing. No scientist of similar stature has come forth in recent years to challenge the acceptance of ESP; to the contrary, more and more universities are devoting departments or special projects to inquire into the field of ESP. What little debunking goes on still is done by inept amateurs trying to hang on to the coat tails of the current occult vogue.

CHAPTER III

WHAT ACTUALLY IS ESP?

ESP may be defined as the ability by individuals to obtain information beyond the limitations of the time–space continuum. In simple terms, the ability to perceive something you couldn't possibly perceive under known laws of cause and effect must be attributed to a different phenomenon, a different power than the one ordinarily in operation with the so-called five senses. Originally, it was thought that it was a separate definite sixth sense (operating) in man, that this sixth sense made it possible for selected individuals to pierce through the time and space barrier on certain occasions and come up with extraordinary results. The idea of a clearly defined separate sixth sense was advanced by the pioneer of parapsychology, Professor Joseph Rhine, whose early experiments at Duke University set the mood and tone for years of experimentation that followed. Professor Rhine investigated the mysterious sixth sense in man following two broad avenues: the ESP factor per se, meaning the ability to circumvent or contradict the time and space laws, and the PSI factor, pertaining to psychokinesis, or the ability to influence solid objects by the power of the mind. Originally, the experiments were initiated by Professor Rhine in association with Dr. Hornell Hart. Later Professor Robert McConnell of the Department of Physics at the University of Pittsburgh conducted similar experiments. Today, Rhine-type experiments are conducted at many universities as the original tests have become almost classical examples of ESP research. In order to test ESP a special deck of cards has been devised by Professor Rhine, with symbols such as squares, circles, and triangles replacing the familiar card illustrations. Those undergoing the test attempt to guess ahead of time the sequence of the cards and over the years many have indeed done so. Despite elaborate studies and impressive statistics, however, the results have remained inconclusive. Not that people have not successfully foretold the exact run of cards in a specific deck, but some very psychic individuals have been total failures in the laboratory while others not so gifted have done extremely well. On the other hand, the same people who failed with the card tests have sometimes had impressive records in the open field with "spontaneous phenomena." Continued testing with cards can be boring; consequently, attention diminishes and the results go down. Without the emotional involvement on the part of the subject, it appears that results cannot really be obtained over any great length of time.

In addition to the card-testing methods, the Rhine laboratory developed PSI machinery to research the potential influence of mind over matter. The fall of dice is used in these experiments to determine the psychic ability of the operator. "In the experiments a man is told which number to wish for to turn up on one or more dice, and the dice are then rolled by machine. The machine devised for just such work by Dr. J. B. Rhine is a cage of transparent material with obstacles in it to make the dice jump around. The cage is turned by a motor and stops by it-self, the only human contact is the hand that flicks the switch to start the motor," explains Monroe Fry in an article entitled "Unsolved Mysteries of Psychic Phenom-ena." The result of years of testing with thousands of sub-jects, varying conditions somewhat, but still insisting on laboratory circumstances and surroundings, led the ex-perimenters to three basic conclusions: (1) in order to have paranormal manifestations, a desire or a need by the subject was of significant importance; (2) ordinary chan-nels of communication would be absent, and (3) there existed no psychological block in the mind of the subject.

Although great numbers of spontaneous cases were brought to the attention of the laboratory at Duke Uni-versity through the years, very little of this material was actually followed up by sending investigators to the places where the phenomena had been observed. This was partly due to lack of funds, of course, but also to a determination on the part of the original investigators to stick to lab-oratory methods and to try to present orthodox scientists with the desired repeatability of psychic phenomena. In the futile search for this ability to repeat phenomena at will in the laboratory, much valuable impetus was lost; in the end, it was clear that the impact of actual phenomena occurring unexpectedly, spontaneously as it were, in the field was much greater than that of artificially produced experiments in the lab. It also became increasingly clear that the rules set up for physical phenomena of other types would not apply to the observation of ESP and PSI phenomena. New rules as well as new tools had to be de-vised to comprehend and understand the vast amount of psychic phenomena presented to science as a new field rather than as a mere branch of orthodox psychology.

ᴬFor one thing, human emotions were always involved. Phenomena did not occur unless someone was deeply involved in their production, consciously or unconsciously, and the absence of the emotional impetus had a marked influence upon the results. Much of the material is stress material and depends for its effectiveness on unique and very real situations; under no circumstances can such conditions be produced in the laboratory except by hypnosis. Even with the use of hypnosis, however, genuine ESP phenomena were not produced in sufficient quantities or at a sufficiently high level to convince scientists already skeptical of the entire field. The more scientists clamored for apparatus and instruments to measure ESP, the more elusive the ability became. Clearly, only the apparatus of the human personality was adequate to serve as a vehicle for the mysterious power. A minority of scientific observers then switched from futile laboratory experiments to actual field observation of phenomena when and if they occurred in such numbers that conclusions could be drawn from them, making possible their investigation.

While American scientists were still debating whether ESP was in fact a real force in man, and, if it was, whether it could be reproduced in laboratory experiments, Russian scientists were way ahead of the game: assuming that ESP existed, they wanted to know how to harness it, how to deal with it, and how to make it work. They were not at all concerned by what method they would reach their goal, and started, so to speak, at the top by using actual sensitives in loosely controlled experiments that were a far

cry from the austere surroundings and clinical atmosphere of the American laboratory. As a result, the Russians
have come up with startling revelations, photographs of
actual psychokinesis in which objects are shown to be
moved a considerable distance by the power of mind, and
they have even initiated more sophisticated experiments,
going beyond ESP into the realm of psychic photography. The recognition of ESP in no way interferes with
their political philosophy: dialectic Marxism may be opposed to the existence of a soul in man, but it seems to be
quite compatible with telepathy and communication between minds, even with communications between the so-
called dead and living and the foretelling of future events.
Although the Russians cling to the notion that there is a
physical base to all ESP faculties, they may in the long run
be on the right track if one considers the physiological
aspects of the phenomena, a matter of degree rather than
of kind.

The very fine elements that make up the channels of
telepathy are in fact physical but of a different density
than the gross physical body of man. ESP, in my view, is
not a separate sixth sense different and apart from the
ordinary five senses. It is, in effect, the ability of man to
go beyond what we currently think are the limits of our
five senses, but which in fact are not. That which we attribute today to a sixth or extra sense may well be considered part of our ordinary five senses in the years to
come. If anything, man has five extra senses; they are the
extra-range of the five senses we generally recognize.
Activated by certain emotional conditions, we are able to
extend our five senses beyond their known boundaries, but
this ability is by no means a freak of nature, an exception

granted by some superior power to a select few or developed only through strenuous and protracted methods. It is the birthright of every one of us, except the mentally incompetent, and it can be dealt with in one of three ways: it can be ignored, it can be suppressed, or it can be enhanced.

If we ignore incidents of ESP in our lives, they will not go away but continue to intrude at various intervals. Ignoring them merely begs the issue: we will remain puzzled by them, perhaps even frightened, and the result will be both unsatisfactory from the point of view of knowledge and from the point of view of a healthy emotional mental outlook.

If we suppress incidents of ESP we may create false personality traits within us. Whether we are motivated by social, religious, or scientific pressures, suppressing genuine incidents of ESP is not conducive to a balanced state of being, nor will it result in the phenomena ceasing altogether. We may suggest to ourselves that invasion from psychic sources is unwanted and undesirable at certain times, and in so doing succeed in closing ourselves off from any and all psychic vibrations or influences, but we cannot do this permanently and on a broad basis. Spontaneous phenomena are bound to occur in our lives from time to time. We cannot possibly prevent them from happening; all we can do if we wish to suppress them is to eliminate our evaluation of the phenomena when they occur, forcing ourselves to look the other way, giving ourselves alternate, safely acceptable explanations for the phenomena occurring within us. In a manner of speaking, then, suppressing ESP incidents is nothing less than the fostering of a falsehood upon ourselves.

Finally, enhancing ESP in ourselves is likely to increase not only the incident rate but also the impact of individual occurrences. The first step toward the encouragement of such phenomena is to accept them as a natural and wholly integrated part of our personalities, something we are born with and something we all ought to have. Our outlook, then, must be directed toward the acceptance of ESP as a natural part of human personality and the absence of ESP as a lack of sorts, making those so afflicted less than perfect individuals. By opening ourselves up to possible incidents, we are actively encouraging their occurrence. We are not manufacturing them nor are we drawing them upon us; ESP phenomena cannot be invoked at the whim of the one desiring to have them occur. They happen when there is a good reason for them to occur. Even telepathic experiments between two subjects are limited in usefulness by the fact that an emotional need has to be present for the phenomena to take place. In the case of experimental attempts, the somewhat limited desire on the part of the experimenters to succeed is sufficient impetus to make the phenomena a success at times but this does not in any way compare to the very real power behind an emergency situation in which telepathy occurs spontaneously.

To define once again the term ESP, we should remember that it is the ability to partake of psychic phenomena of all kinds.

Anyone having a psychic experience, even once in a lifetime, has ESP.

Anyone called psychic or mediumistic or a sensitive has ESP.

Anyone obtaining specific information on events or individuals with whom he is not familiar in his conscious state has ESP.

Anyone obtaining glimpses into the so-called future or past without consciously being able to do so shows evidence of ESP.

Knowledge obtained that cannot be explained reasonably or adequately by the ordinary five senses must be attributed to extrasensory perception. Of course, this knowledge must be specific, reasonably detailed, and not of the kind that could be attributed to background information available to the subject, not even to knowledge available to another individual in the presence of the subject, since telepathic transfer of information is a distinct possibility.

There does not seem to be a marked difference between the dimension of time and the dimension of space as far as the ability of man to pierce it is concerned. In a way, both dimensions are alike. By the same token, there does not seem to be any difference between ESP into the future and ESP into the past. As a matter of fact, the dimension of time may be altogether absent and what we are dealing with is in effect an accommodation to make the dimension commonly called time more feasible to our way of reckoning. This is even more borne out by the fact that events seem to be stationary in this time-like dimension and it is we who move toward events, at which moment they occur to us.

ESP phenomena are part of "mental" phenomena. Psychic research divides phenomena into mental and physical phenomena. Mental phenomena include clairvoyance, clairaudience, clairsentience, telepathy, and psychometry. ESP is the driving force in all of these. The "physical" phenomena, principally trance and materializations, do not come under the heading of ESP phenomena but ESP may be present in all such manifestations. The driving force in physical phenomena, however, is psychokinesis, a physical force, rather than the purely mental force responsible for ESP phenomena.

Clairvoyance is the ability to "see clear," that is, beyond the boundaries of time and space. It applies equally to seeing into the future and seeing into the past. It applies, of course, also to seeing into a distance away from oneself and observing occurrences going on either simultaneously, in the past, or in the future. Some phenomena of this kind involve both distance in time and space, others merely one of the two.

Clairaudience is the phenomenon of hearing sounds, such as voices, not emanating from visible sources in the immediate vicinity of the percipient. Auditory phenomena may be from the present, from the past, or from the "future"; they may occur in the immediate vicinity of the observer or over a long distance. Phenomena of this category may be a combination of one or several possibilities. The incidence rate of clairvoyance is much higher than that of clairaudience.

Least frequent is the phenomenon called clairsentience, one form of which is the registration of specific scents for which there appears to be no logical reason. These scents represent associations both with people and with places and in this manner communicate certain meanings to the recipient. They may be from the past, present, or so-called future, or they may be from a distance, just as the other three forms of ESP. However, due to the limits imposed by the nature of odors, clairsentience alone is not significant in the understanding of material and is usually a secondary manifestation along with clairaudience or clairvoyance. However, it follows the same channels and is activated by ESP precisely the way clairvoyance or clairaudience is.

᾿ Psychometry is the ability to derive information from the touch of objects. This is based on the theory that emotional events create a thin film that coats all objects, including people, in the immediate vicinity of the occurrence. This coating of objects or people is permanent and does not dissipate, except in a very minute way of little significance to us in our lives. A psychometrist coming in contact with such objects or individuals will be able to read the coating substance and thus will be able to reconstruct the emotional event. Most psychometry concerns the past, some of it bears on the present, and occasionally psychometric readings pertain to the so-called future. Some individuals need to touch an object that has been on the person of one who is about to be investigated, while others get stimuli from being in the immediate vicinity of the person, without, however, touching him. Psychometry has been used successfully by professional mediums to locate lost persons by the medium touching an object belonging to the person and reconstructing his immediate past. In some, as yet little understood, fashion, inducing agents such as personal possessions may also result in projections into the future of the owner, thus making psychometry useful in crime prevention and other branches of detective work.

᾿Telepathy or mind-to-mind communication is probably

the best-known form of ESP. It works primarily between living people but is certainly the base of alleged communications with the dead as well. Telepathic thoughts or images are transferred from one mind to the other. The message is encoded, sent through space at great speed, received by the mind of the recipient, decoded, and brought to consciousness. The entire process is almost simultaneous, although some time does elapse. Since we are dealing here with tiny amounts of electromagnetic energies, actually transmitted through space and thus traveling from one person to another, some "time" must of necessity elapse. But the amount of time is so infinitesimal that it appears to be simultaneous transmission. More than any branch of ESP, telepathy is capable of inducement, that is to say, willful attempts to make it work. In many ways it resembles radio transmissions. The strong desire of the experimenter to succeed is frequently sufficient impetus to make the telepathic communication succeed. Depending upon the relationship between sender and receiver, the communication may be partial or complete. The closer the emotional ties between the two individuals concerned, the more likely that the results will be satisfactory. "Being in tune" is not a mere figure of speech, but a very real condition enhancing telepathic communication.

The difference between clairvoyance in the present, even at a distance, and telepathy is slight. The two forms of ESP overlap. However, clairvoyance is never induced, always spontaneous, while telepathy can be induced or planned. When telepathy is spontaneous, that is, unexpected, it differs from clairvoyance in that thoughts are being transmitted from another mind. With clairvoyance, visual imprints are received; in clairaudience, spoken words or noises are received, but in telepathy thoughts are received.

Man is either asleep or awake. The sleep state represents roughly one third of the time spent on the physical plane. In the sleep state the bonds of consciousness are loosened and the ties between conscious and unconscious minds are sometimes very, very slight. In this condition, it is easier for telepathic material to enter the unconscious mind of the receiver than when he is awake. Consequently, much ESP material enters the receiver during the sleep state. The advantage of this entry is that the obstacle of the conscious mind is removed, thus more of the message can be absorbed. The disadvantage is that, upon awakening, the receiver may have forgotten part of the message, or personal dream material of a symbolic or psychoanalytic nature may intrude upon the ESP material, become mixed up with it, or in some way alter the purity of the impression. We do not have much control over the way we receive ESP material from others; to send material while asleep has thus far proven to be impossible. Despite some extraordinary happenings indicating a close relationship between thoughts and actual physical action, ESP does not make people act in certain patterns or cause things to occur. Indirectly, ESP may cause people to receive certain thoughts or impulses and then react to them, but we do not have the power over others via the ESP route the way hypnotists may temporarily hold power over a hypnotized subject. ESP is both a power and channel of communication. It has many facets and forms of appearance, and it works best on the unconscious level.

What makes it operate is similar to electromagnetic current, and it thus depends upon a sufficient supply of that energy in the sender, and to a lesser degree in the recipient. Like all psychic force, however, frequent use of ESP powers does not deplete the individual but in some, as yet not fully understood, way helps replenish the supply of psychic energies. The more we use ESP, the more we have. Above all, ESP is not a miraculous power given to a few chosen ones; ESP is not something you can buy or acquire in mind-study courses alone; it is a natural facet of human personality inherent in everyone, frequently left dormant because it is not always fully understood. Its development should be taught in schools the way the three R's are, and perhaps in the not too distant future it will be. Whatever else ESP may be, it most certainly is not *super*natural.

CHAPTER IV

CAN WE FORETELL THE FUTURE?

Perhaps the most tantalizing aspect of ESP is its application to the foretelling of future events. It stands to reason that nothing interests a person more than to know what lies ahead, whether for himself or for the community in which he lives, whether for a loved one or simply in terms of general world conditions. The forbidden is always most attractive. Forbidden in this respect does not mean that there attaches anything evil or unsavory to foreknowledge of the future, nor does any religious faith forbid it. What references there are in the Bible to mediumship, generally based upon misinterpretations or mistranslations of ancient Greek terminology, refer to the consulting with mediums rather than the talent of foreseeing the future. The prophets of the Old Testament were held in high esteem and the gift of prophecy was always held to be divinely inspired.

Nothing matters more than knowledge of what lies ahead, since it covers conditions that have not yet come to pass so that there is the possibility of preparing for them in one way or another. Knowledge of contemporary events, even if they transpire at a distance in space, are less dramatic. True, Swedenborg told his audience of the great fire of Stockholm while hundreds of miles away and while the fire was actually going on. The effect was most dramatic, but his audience also realized that there was little if anything they could do about the event itself and it would take some time before the truth of Swedenborg's statements could be confirmed. As it was, he had been entirely correct in his visionary experience.

Delving into the past and describing conditions with which one is not normally familiar may be related to the ability to foretell the future in terms of technical procedure, but in terms of human interest it does not rank as high as the quest for tomorrow. This is, of course, simply due to man's greater interest in what lies ahead than that which has already become part of his experience. Quite definitely, we cannot alter past events. We may be able to change our attitudes toward them, but that implies personal changes rather than changes of events that have already transpired. We may be able to make some adjustments to events while they are going on, such as news of an earthquake occurring at a distance out of expectation that it may eventually hit us also, but in general the only area where we can take action based upon ESP foreknowledge lies with the ability to foretell future events.

There is still another aspect that makes the ability to foretell future events more controversial and tantalizing than any other aspect of ESP. An event that has not yet come into being is something that the ordinary person cannot perceive or even conceive, something that does not exist and has no reality. Yet, hundreds of thousands of people are able to describe in great detail situations and happenings that come to pass only at a later date. If this is true—and research has amply borne it out—then our concept of time and the sequence of events are subject to revision. Quite clearly, if people in significant numbers can foresee and foretell future events far beyond the law of chance and far beyond guesswork or generalities, then either our sense of time is wrong or the events themselves are predestined by some superior law with which we are not yet fully familiar. It is very difficult to judge such matters from within the same dimension and it is quite impossible for anyone to be totally outside it at any time. One must therefore construct a theory that would satisfy the existence of many such experiences pertaining to the so-called future, while at the same time satisfying our basic three-dimensional concepts of life on earth and the established view of the time-space continuum. I will examine the nature of time in a later chapter, but for purposes of this aspect of ESP, let it be stated that time is a human convenience, adopted in order to have a reference point; events are indeed predestined to a large degree by a system that I prefer to call the Universal Law. About this also more anon.

Precognition is the ability to know beforehand, to have accurate information about events, situations, and people ahead of the time that we become consciously aware of them. The majority of precognitive experiences occur spontaneously and unsought. Some people may have an inkling of a precognitive situation shortly before it occurs by feeling odd, experiencing a sensation of giddiness or tingling in various parts of the body, or simply a vague foreboding that a psychic experience is about to take place. To others, these things come entirely out of left field, surprisingly and certainly unexpectedly. Many find the ability to foretell future events more of a burden than a blessing because they begin to believe that foretelling bad events may in some way be connected with their causing them. This, of course, is not true. By tuning into the existing conditions and through ESP picking up that which lies ahead, the receiver is merely acting as a channel without responsibility to the event itself, the outcome, the timing, the result of the event, or the moral implications of it. He has no more control over that which he foretells than a radio set has control over programing coming through it. I have a number of letters from people who think that they are "evil witches" because they have foreseen an accident or death of a friend or loved one and had it happen exactly as they had foreseen it. They wonder whether their thoughts have caused the event to occur, especially in cases where there has been an unpleasant relationship between the psychic and the victim. There are cases on record where thought concentrations may cause people to be influenced at a distance, may even make them do certain things that are not consciously in their will, but this requires a conscious and deliberate effort, usually several people working together, and lacks the spontaneity of ESP flashes generally associated with true precognitive experiences.

Actually, the ability to look into the future is a tightly knit and progressive ability in every one of us, starting with primitive instincts, when man senses danger or love or warmth and reacts accordingly, through intuition in which his inner voice warns him of danger or somehow vaguely makes him react with caution against dangerous individuals or situations, to the higher stage of the "hunch" where actual ESP begins. A hunch is a basically illogical feeling about a person or situation that influences one's thinking and actions. Following a hunch means to go against purely logical reasoning. If the hunch turns out to be correct, one has had a mild ESP experience. If the hunch turns out to be false, it may not have been a hunch at all but fear. The two are very much alike. Fear of failure, fear of a confrontation that is undesirable may frequently masquerade as a hunch. The only way to tell the two apart is the sense of immediacy, the sudden appearance and the short duration of the true hunch, whereas fear is a lingering and generally somewhat extended feeling. Beyond the simple hunch there lies the ability to foresee or foretell actual events or situations. This ability is called precognition, meaning foreknowledge. Whether the foreknowledge is of events that occur one minute later or a year afterward is of no importance. The technique involved is exactly the same since we are dealing here with a dimension in which time, as we define it, does not exist. The precognitive process goes through a variety of stages or degrees.

There is, first of all, the situation where one foresees or foretells an encounter with either a situation or a person without "getting" any specifics as to time and place, mainly receiving only the basic message. When this simple precognitive experience occurs in the dream or sleep state it may be surrounded by, or couched in, symbolic language, in which case parallel situations may well masquerade as the message itself. For instance, you may have a precognitive dream about your brother having bought a new car that he wants to show you. The following day there is a phone call from him advising you that he is going to visit you in the near future. When he arrives, it turns out that he has just remarried and wants you to meet his bride. The car of the dream experience was the symbol for the new wife. In the waking condition, however, descriptive material is much more precise, and even though not every precognitive experience contains the desired details of time, place, and description, the absence of the material from the unconscious mind allows the message to be much clearer and more precise.

Next comes the precognitive impression where a time or place element is concluded; this may be only partial, such as a numeral "flashed" above the face of someone who appears as a precognitive vision. Or it may be a key word spoken by an inner voice that relates to the circumstances under which the precognitive experience will take place. Depending upon the individual personality of the receiver and his state of relaxation at the time of the experience, the precognitive message will either be partial or more involved. If the material is merely routine although of some emotional significance to the receiver, it is less likely to contain dramatic descriptive material than if we are dealing with catastrophes, warning of dire events, or precognitive material of importance to more than one individual. Those who are able to foretell plane crashes, for instance, which is a specialty among some clairvoyants, do so with a great deal of detail; fires and earthquakes also seem to evoke graphic response in the ESP consciousness of those able to foretell them. The curious thing, of course, is that not all such occurrences take place as predicted. This, however, is not due to the inaccuracy of the vision or precognitive experience, but to the total lack on the part of the visionary as to correct judgment of the time element, coming as it does from a timeless dimension. There remains the question whether the person with ESP ability foresees the future around a specific individual or independent of that individual. If a number of precognitive predictions are made about one individual by a number of seers independent of each other, then the future event must cling to the aura or electromagnetic field of the individual about whom the predictions are made. If, on the other hand, individuals foretell such events in the future about an individual without being in that individual's presence, then a channel into the future itself seems to have been opened in which the individual who is concerned with those events merely plays a part and a part over which he has no control.

Anyone doubting the factuality of precognition need only consult the records of psychical research societies throughout the world for detailed descriptions of cases, carefully recorded by them over the years.

Premonitions are a milder form of precognitive experiences in the sense that they are usually feelings about events to come rather than sharply defined flashes of actual scenes. Premonitions are much more numerous than the more complex form of precognitive experience. Theodore Irwin, in an article entitled "Can Some People See Into the Future?" published in *Family Weekly*, May 4, 1969, reports on the strong premonition by a London piano teacher named Lorna Middleton concerning the fate of Senator Robert Kennedy. Nine months before the assassination, Mrs. Middleton felt a strong premonition that he would be murdered. On March 15 of the year in which Kennedy died she actually saw the assassination take place and felt it was while the senator was on tour in the West. This impression was followed by another one on April 5 and again on April 11 when she had a foreboding of death connected with the Kennedy family. The actual murder took place on June 5.

As a result of peoples' premonitions frequently reported in the press, a psychiatrist named Dr. R. D. Barker set up a Central Premonitions Registry where people could register their premonitory feelings toward the day when their impressions might become reality. The greatest impetus toward some sort of registration of the phenomena the project received was in October of 1966 when a huge coal tip buried the Welsh Village of Aberfan, killing 138 children and adults in the process. Many people in Britain reported premonitions concerning the event, some even giving exact data as to when and how the disaster would occur. Among those who had an inkling of the catastrophe was my good friend Michael Bentine, the writer and comedian, who had scheduled a TV sketch dealing with a Welsh village on the fatal day. For reasons unknown to him, however, he canceled this particular sketch at the last minute.

Dr. Barker thought of the registry not only as an instrument to prove scientifically that people do foretell the future, but as a kind of clearing house to warn of impending catastrophes. To do so, of course, it was necessary to prove that a significant percentage of the premonitions were actually coming true. A study of premonitions filed with the registry during the year 1967 disclosed 469 separate entries. Only eighteen of these proved to be accurate, and of those, twelve were made by only two individuals, the aforementioned Miss Middleton and Allen P. Hencher, a forty-five-year-old telephone worker.

"They are absolutely genuine," Dr. Barker is quoted in

Family Weekly. "Quite honestly they stagger me. Somehow these sensitive people can gate-crash the time barrier —see the wheels of disaster starting to turn before the rest of us. It is difficult to attribute their experiences to coincidence alone."

Taking a lead from the British doctor, several Americans have also attempted to set up premonition registries. Among them is Dr. Stanley Krippner, clinical psychologist and director of the Dream Laboratory at Maimonides Medical Center, Brooklyn. A young man named Richard Nelson, part of a twin team of sensitives, also has set up a registry of this kind. Unfortunately, the majority of people with premonitory experiences never bother to register them with anyone. I myself receive a fair number of such claims, but only a fraction of the number that actually transpire. This is, of course, due to the fact that most premonitions concern disaster or negative aspects of life. People are afraid to bring bad news and frequently prefer to dismiss the impressions or actively suppress them. As a result, much valuable psychic material is undoubtedly lost to science, and where there might have been warnings, and possibly prevention of disaster, there is only the *fait accompli.*

Allen Hencher, one of the two British sensitives, is quoted as saying, "Most of the premonitions come while I am working, maybe because there is a lot of electricity at the telephone switchboard, yet they also come at night, when the air is clear, or after a glass of wine. Usually my premonitions are accompanied by headaches, like a steel band around my forehead, but as I write them down, the headaches recede. When I feel that a premonition has been borne out, I feel utter relief. It is as if something had been bottled up in me."

Probably the most surprising premonition recorded by Mr. Hencher, which was quoted widely in the British press at the time, was a hunch relating to an airplane accident. He had been awake all night due to the ominous headache and during that period clearly foresaw an airplane crash in which there would be 124 victims. He described the scene as reminding him of Greece and detailed some statuary around a church when he telephoned Dr. Barker with his report the following morning. Instinctively, Mr. Hencher felt that he was referring to Cyprus. Several weeks later there was indeed an airplane crash on Cyprus in which 124 people were killed.

Dr. Stanley Kripper of Maimonides Hospital, Brooklyn, is quoted as saying, "Our notion of the dividing line between present and future is probably incorrect. We interpret the present as being the exact moment when something is going on. In reality, however, the present for an event may come within a wider span of time. There are forces at work now that will probably not become obvious for a year or two. Then, when an event does take place, in retrospect we realize that it is part of the present."

Helen Ann Elsner of Iowa has worked as a nurse's aide in various hospitals and currently is a laboratory assistant in animal science. Her paranormal occurrences usually take the form of premonitory dreams. As a child she had had a recurrent dream in which she saw a specific drugstore and a dime store in a town she was not familiar with. When she was staying in Grand Falls, Canada, in the summer of 1958, she suddenly recalled those dreams. She felt compelled to walk into the town and to her surprise found the specific two stores she had so often seen in her dreams. From that moment on the dream ceased. As a child she had dreamed also about a three-story mansion with a long curved stairway leading into the main living room. Years later she found herself in Lowell, Massachusetts, as a missionary student. The house she went to live in was that house, exactly as she had seen it years before in her dreams. In the summer of 1961, Miss Elsner was stationed at Fort Belvoir, Virginia, as a medical corpsman of the Women's Army Corps. In the cafeteria of the military hospital she met a young man named Jackson, a fellow corpsman. About two months later she had a dream about him that stayed vividly in her mind. In the dream she saw Jackson in patient's pajamas and felt that she was the hospital aide taking care of him. She saw herself straightening the covers of his bed as part of the evening care when he reached up and tried to kiss her. At that moment a lady walked into the room. She heard Jackson remark, "There's my ex-wife. I did not know she knew where I was, let alone sick, because we are divorced." On that note the dream ended. Several weeks later when she came to the cafeteria, she saw Jackson in hospital pajamas and immediately recalled her dream. He asked her to come to his ward. As she was standing by his bed and talking about a book she had read, Jackson looked up and interrupted their conversation with the comment, "There is my ex-wife. I didn't know she knew where I was, let alone sick, because we are divorced." How could Miss Elsner have guessed or in any way foretold the exact words spoken on that occasion, especially as she lacked the fundamental knowledge concerning Mr. Jackson?

Only by tapping the so-called future can we explain incidents of this kind, which are indeed numerous. Sometimes the ESP apparatus projects events at a limited distance in both space and time. In November of 1972, Miss Elsner was driving home from work at about six in the evening. When she neared Twenty-fourth Street in the town of Ames, she could not get it out of her mind that there would be an accident scene ahead. She took this as a warning and became a very cautious driver for the next few blocks. When she got to Twenty-fourth Street there was the scene she had pictured in her mind: two wrecked cars, three police cars, and an ambulance.

Miss Elsner has learned to live with her gift. Her ESP not only warns her of disaster but can be used for minor worldly pursuits as well. The trouble is that she has very little control over it. "Sometimes when I am shopping I get that certain feeling or urge to go to a certain store for whatever it is I want. Sometimes I have to look for a long time in that store, but I have always found the article. The sad part is that this feeling is not voluntary, it comes only when it wishes, and if I push the issue I may go wrong," she explains.

Mrs. Barbara Moeller works as an office manager for a painting and decorating company in Omaha, Nebraska. She is genuinely psychic and has valid experiences with haunted houses as well as communications with the alleged dead. "My experiences in precognition are many," she says. "Once I had a strange dream in which I was driving either to or from work along a narrow street from my business place to the main artery. I saw very clearly

how my car hit a small boy. I saw the boy's boot fly in the
air and a profusion of blood stream down his face. I am
a very careful driver so this dream bothered me greatly. I
confided in my husband and also a cousin and revealed
the dream to them several weeks prior to it becoming
reality. For several weeks I watched very carefully as I
drove along this particular street. Finally, one day when
I was absolutely not thinking about the accident and was
approaching the area of my dream, a young boy darted
from between a car and a truck. Immediately I applied my
brakes, but too late. I had struck the boy and just as in the
dream he lost his boot and his nose bled profusely. Even
though I had been forewarned, I was greatly upset. Fortunately, the boy was not seriously injured."

Mrs. Kaye Schoerning of Oklahoma has a long record
of ESP experiences. When she still lived with her family at
Hillsboro, Texas, where she was working as a nurse, her
family owned a hotel that had a Western Union agency.
One day she read in the local newspaper that three gunmen had robbed a Sears store to the southwest. That night
she dreamed the same men would come the following
day at exactly 12:00 A.M. to rob their local Sears store. In
the morning the agency received a telegram from the
Sears district manager warning them of the three men and
to be on the lookout for them. Since Mrs. Schoerning's
father was also mayor of the town, she took the telegram
to him and asked him to do something about it. At the
same time, she informed him of her premonitory dream.
Her father shook his head. Why would three gunmen
want to rob such a small store? But when she insisted, he
called the police in. At exactly 12:00 A.M. the three men

appeared at the store and tried to rob it. Because of the warning, however, the police captured the thieves and Mrs. Schoerning's dream proved to be entirely accurate.

Although it is impossible to channel one's ESP powers to guarantee the desired results, especially in dreams, sometimes dream material of a very mundane nature may come to the surface.

J. Hugh Smith owns real estate and plays the stock market in Missouri. He is in his late thirties, divorced, and has three sons. Premonitory dreams have come to him all his life. "I recently dreamed that a stock I owned, Standard Motor Products, would reach twenty-three and a half and then back off. In the dream I was unable to be at the broker's to act in time and I remember the broker telling me about it going to that price. Shortly afterward it hit twenty-one and one half and backed off, but I was out of town and the words my broker used in telling me were the same ones as in the dream," he explained.

Mary Pugar of Oregon has had a series of premonitory experiences, mainly in the dream state. "The very first such dream I had was in North Dakota when I was about eight years old," she told me. "One night I dreamed I was pulling the curtain of the window where my mother was sleeping. Then suddenly the large curtain pole came down with a crash, almost killing her. Forty-two years later, when I was teaching in central Oregon, an incident occurred which brought that dream back to me. I was just about to leave for school when mother said she was going to go to the woodshed to get some wood. I put my books down and said I would go to get it for her. I had just started to pull the shed door open when a slight sound made me hesitate. The next thing I knew a heavy two-by-four over the door fell down in front of me. In that instant I recalled that dream. If mother had gone out she would not have hesitated but would have gone right in, since she was hard of hearing and would not have heard the slight sound."

Some professional mediums have made almost a career out of predicting catastrophes. Shawn Robbins, a young lady I have personally trained as a medium, has an impressive accuracy record in the prediction of airplane crashes.

John Gaudry, a young man who has worked with me on several occasions, gave me a written statement on January 20, 1971, concerning a dream he had had the night before. "I saw a rather large helicopter crash into cold waters, either a bay or river. It was painted either orange or red and was a cabin-type helicopter. People were splashing around in the water but seemed to be able to make it. I fear this may happen within the next few days and within the New York area." According to the New York *Daily News* of January 24, 1971, four days later, a helicopter piloted by Apollo 14 backup pilot Eugene Cernan crashed with terrific impact into a river and burst into flames while the astronaut was making simulated lunar landings. Cernan was picked up by one of several passing boats and was rushed to a nearby marina. Later he was examined by space agency physician Dr. John Teegen and was pronounced unhurt. Although John Gaudry was wrong about the area in which the ac-

cident was to occur, he had described the scene pretty
accurately.

Is there any training we can use to enhance our ability
to foretell the future? First of all, people who have had
some indication of this talent would naturally be more
likely to be able to do something about increasing it than
those who come to it cold. But the technique to be used
is pretty much the same in either case. Basically, it consists of a state of watchfulness toward any indication, no
matter how slight, that a premonition is about to take
place. Nothing must be ignored; everything should be
written down and, if possible, reputable witnesses should
be alerted as to the nature of the premonition as soon as
it is received. If possible, one should write oneself a letter
concerning the experience and mail it by registered
mail to oneself, thus permitting the postmark to act as a
guarantee concerning the time element of the prediction.
As to increasing one's ability to have premonitory experiences, the attitude should be one of acceptance, regard-
less of whether the material to be obtained is pleasant or
unpleasant. Absence of fear and a certain objectivity concerning the material are equally necessary. Morally one
is required to pass on whatever information is received,
whether it is good or bad. If specific information concerning the future is wanted, there are certain inducing
agents that may work. If the subject is someone other than
oneself, perhaps a photograph or the person's name written in clear letters on a piece of paper may serve as a
concentration point. Having visualized the subject or object of the search into the future, one settles back in as
relaxed a state as possible and concentrates upon the sub-

ject or object. In this respect the process resembles meditation except that a precise channeling is taking place.
Tangent thoughts should be dismissed, and the mind, if
wandering off, should be disciplined to stick to the topic
at hand. Another approach might be to go to a place, a
house or some other location about which one seeks to obtain precognitive material. One might then gather impressions about it, although this is primarily of a psychometric
nature. Only when being on location triggers a true precognitive experience, spontaneous and unexpectedly, will
this work and fall properly in the area of this chapter. By
and large, precognitive experiences come to one unsought
and unexpectedly. In sharpening one's general ESP abilities and streamlining one's concepts about it, one contributes indirectly to the greater frequency of spontaneous premonitions.

When precognitive experiences reach major proportions
and involve large segments of the population, even entire
countries, we speak of prophecy. The advantage of such
material is that it is of interest to a much larger group of
people than personal predictions or premonitions. The
disadvantage, of course, is that public figures and problems are involved about which almost everyone has at
least a degree of conscious knowledge. Thus the annual
ritual of predicting future events in the year ahead so dear
to the heart of journalists is nothing more than a farce.
Since they ask a group of mediumistic people selected at
random, usually in brief telephone interviews, the predictions given to the journalists are indeed vague and general. It is not too difficult to make some sort of fitting prediction about Mrs. Kennedy or President Nixon or Mao.

As a matter of fact, in collecting material for an earlier book entitled *The Prophets Speak*, I discarded much of this kind of material because it was simply too broad and too vaguely worded.

Whenever predictions concerning public figures are made, the researchers should insist on specific details of dates, places, and circumstances. If possible, aspects of a public figure that are not generally known should be involved. Perhaps the most classic example is the record of the French seer Michael Nostradamus, a sixteenth-century physician who enjoyed the confidence of the French kings. His predictions were couched in poetic language and written in quatrains as a matter of safety at a time when witches were still being put to death and anyone possessed of ESP was considered a witch. Nostradamus went on record in the 1560s as predicting that there would be a king of France named Henry IV who would be assassinated on a certain French highway by a schoolteacher whose name Nostradamus also gave. The assassination took place as described some fifty years later. At the time when Nostradamus made his prediction neither the king nor the murderer had yet been born.

Nostradamus speaks of submarines, atomic warfare, and airplanes as if he knew these machines intimately. In his predictions for the future yet to come in our lives, he speaks of a terrible great war after which there would be a "government of England from America." This statement was made at the time when the term "America" had not yet come into being. Since Nostradamus has also identified Adolf Hitler correctly by name and has given the correct description of what transpired during Hitler's time, students of prophecy should take the French seer's predictions very seriously in relating them to events yet to come.

The answer, then, to the question as to whether we can foretell the future must be in the affirmative; at the same time, we should realize that we cannot turn this faculty on at will nor can we regulate it even partially. At best, we can observe it competently and draw certain conclusions from it, not so much about ourselves, but about the nature of the so-called future and our role in the scheme of things.

CHAPTER V

CAN WE WALK INTO THE PAST?

Just as the future, which is not yet when viewed from the present, so the past is no more when seen from the same vantage point. Although artifacts may be standing from distant periods in the past, the past itself is gone. The events shaping it and the people in it are no longer in existence in the physical sense of the word. There is, however, one basic difference between the past and the future. The future is not yet, when seen from the present, and therefore has no realistic existence in terms of the ordinary five senses. The past, on the other hand, has existed already and therefore does have a track record of having been at one time. The difficulty in coming to terms with these expressions lies not so much in the limitations of our ordinary five senses as in the terminology we are forcing ourselves to use. By dividing our consciousness into three distinct segments—past, present, and future—we are arbitrarily cutting a steady flow of consciousness into separate and distinct units. In actuality, the progression from past to present to future is continuous and uninterrupted. It is also relative to the observer, that is to say the present of now becomes the past of now plus one. The past is nothing more than the present gone on. In essence, past, present, and future are made of the same stuff. The dividers are artificial and flexible. The only proof that something has become objective reality, that is to say has already happened, comes from observation of the event. If we were not there to notice it, the event itself would transpire just the same, even though there would be no witnesses to record it. When we thus speak of the past, it is to be taken as subjective in the sense that it is the past as seen from our individual points of view. These individual points of view may be similar among most people, but they are nevertheless nothing more than the sum total of individual observations and reflect the past only because the observers are at a later juncture in time than the observed event. Perhaps it would be more correct to speak of such events as accomplished events rather than past events.

By contrast, future events could be characterized as unrealized events. The reality of the events would be identical; only their relationship to the observer would differ. From the point of view of the observer, past events have occurred and can no longer be altered. Future events, on the other hand, exist independently but have not yet occurred in relationship to the observer and may conceivably be altered, at least in some instances.

There are several ways in which we can actually transport ourselves, or anyway parts of ourselves, into the so-called past.

In psychometry we derive impressions from an object, from a person, or from a place about events that have taken place sometime before our experiment. These impressions are always emotionally tinged. Purely logical material does not seem to survive. The outburst of emotional energy whenever traumatic events occur furnishes the raw material with which objects, people, or places are coated and which contains the memory banks of the events themselves. In touching an object or person or being in the immediate vicinity of the event, we are merely replaying it the way a phonograph replays a prerecorded record. The events themselves do not possess any active life and the reproduction is quite faithful, subject only to the limitations of the transmission and the personality traits of the receiver. Therefore, the message may contain part or all of the original event, it may come through correctly or partially correctly, or it may be a mixture of event and personal interpretation, since, after all, the receiver is human and not a machine. But the process itself is basically an impersonal one; it should work equally well, no matter what the occasion or where the location of the experiment is.

In psychometry, then, we read a kind of emotional photograph of past events. In reconstructing it through the psychometric impulses and with the help of our conscious mind, we are not actually re-creating the event itself but merely an imprint or copy of it. This, however, is sufficient to derive information about an event and thus learn facts that may otherwise be lost in history. Some years ago, in a book entitled *Window to the Past,* I showed how a medium can be taken to historical "hot" spots, places where puzzles in history have not been fully resolved, and attempt psychometry to resolve pending issues. Mrs. Sybil Leek was thus able to pinpoint the actual location of Camelot in England and of the first Viking landings on Cape Cod in Massachusetts. ESP in this application is a valid and very valuable tool of historical exploration and can undoubtedly be used much more than it has been in the past, when all other means of historical research fail. To be sure, the information obtained in this manner is by no means used verbatum to correct missing parts of history but is used only as a departure point for research in conventional ways.

A second method of visiting the past is astral projection, also called "out-of-the-body experiences," in which our inner self, the etheric body, leaves the physical abode temporarily and travels, usually at great speeds. Ordinarily, astral projection is in space rather than in time. It is, however, quite possible to direct one's astral projection into a predetermined segment of past history. It works better if done at the location one aims to investigate, but can also be done a distance away from it. The success will depend upon the power of visualization by the subject, and the absence of interference from conscious or unconscious sources. Induced astral projection should not be undertaken alone but only in the presence of a competent observer. The subject, who should have a history of past astral travel, will then suggest, or have suggested to him, that travel into a particular region of space and time is requested and that all the information obtained once one gets there should be recalled upon return and awakening. Somewhere on the borderline between astral projection and psychometry lies what the late Eileen Garrett called "traveling clairvoyance." In traveling clairvoyance part of the medium is projected outward and is able to observe conditions as they existed in the past without actually leaving the physical body. This, however, is a talent found primarily in professional mediums and those with a great deal of experience in controlling their phases of mediumship. It is not an easily acquired talent. In any event, astral projection is accomplished by lying on a comfortable surface, preferably at a time of day when the body is reasonably tired and relaxed, and by gently suggesting an outward motion of the inner etheric body. Closing one's eyes while suggesting to oneself the loosening of the bonds between conscious and unconscious minds initiates an outward floating, which will eventually become a physical sensation. The inner self may leave the physical body through the upper solar plexus, at the top of the head or through the stomach area. Return is accompanied by a sensation of rapid deceleration, experienced as a kind of free fall, a spinning and occasionally an unpleasant feeling of having fallen from great heights. This, however, is due only to the rapid change of speed between the etheric body and the physical body. The adjustment is undertaken in a comparatively short time and can therefore be momentarily unpleasant, but is in no way representative of danger to either body or mind.

Hypnotic regression, as it is used in connection with reincarnation research, also propels the individual into the past. Such experiments, always undertaken under the supervision of a professional hypnotist trained in parapsychology, may result in the obtaining of information from past incarnations and can be verified independently afterward. With regression it is always best to suggest to the subject that the past memory will not be retained upon awakening in order to avoid any traumatic residue. Thus, the only information about the past available to the researcher is that which the hypnotized subject brings while in the hypnotized state. Since hypnotic regression is

more concerned with personal experiences in past lives
rather than with historical exploration, the thrust of the
investigation is somewhat different from that required for
purely past-oriented research.

There are a number of instances on record where people have accidently entered a "time warp," that is to say
areas in which a different time stream was still extant.

One such case concerns a young man who drove from
northern Oregon to California and suddenly found himself at the bend of a road in a blizzard, although he had
left in August when the weather was extremely hot. For
what seemed to him a full day he found himself in a min-
ing town among people dressed in clothes of the early
1900s. He remembers vividly having spoken to them and
found them to be three-dimensional people. Suddenly he
was seized by panic and, regaining the safety of his automobile, drove away, to the bewilderment of the entities
he left behind. Shortly afterward, he found himself back
again in the present and the relative comforts of a hot
August day.

One must not classify such experiences as hallucinations, even though hallucinations are possibile with certain individuals. With cases of this kind, the material
obtained during the incident is the crux of the explanation: in the case of the young man, detailed descriptions
of his encounter seem to indicate that he did indeed enter
a time warp of sorts. Whether this was due to his own
mediumistic abilities or to the location at which he encountered the phenomenon is difficult to assess. But similar cases have been reported from time to time where
people, and even vehicles, from the past have been ob-

served amid contemporary scenes, only to vanish a few moments later or to return on other occasions or to other observers. Scenes from the past are not unlike ghosts except that ghosts are tied to specific locations and personal fates whereas these scenes seem to exist independently and encompass a variety of individual people within them. Why some of these scenes from the past "hang around" while the majority have faded away, we do not as yet know. In all cases known to me, however, there have been emotional connotations involved, and I thus feel that unresolved emotional problems may be at the base of keeping such scenes in existence. Perhaps someday we will devise an apparatus to replay historical occurrences at will.

Albert Einstein has pointed out that energy cannot dissipate but must continue to exist even if it is transmuted or otherwise changed in form. Could it not be that the emotionally tinged scenes, which, after all, represent energy, exist in a dimension not ordinarily accessible to us for observation? On occasion, however, specific individuals are able to penetrate into this dimension where past events continue to move on a different time track from the one we have created for our own convenience.

Thus, walking into the past is both a matter of choice and a matter of accident. Either way, the past is far from dead and continues to intermingle with our present. Probably the most common form of "reading" the past history of a person or a place is the kind of ESP that permits one to tell facts about such a person or place without having access to any information or any previous conscious knowledge of the person or place. Since this is a very common talent, it must be assumed that the past continues to exist all around us, that is to say exudes tiny particles of itself so that those sufficiently sensitive to it may derive information from the emanations.

CHAPTER VI

ESP AND THE DEAD

Many scientifically minded individuals will readily accept the reality of ESP while at the same time strenuously objecting to the possibility of survival of human personality beyond physical death. Whereas ESP, to them at least, indicates an extraordinary faculty between individuals, the idea of an existence beyond death involves a religious concept, to some people enough of a deterrent to look the other way even in the face of considerable evidence.

Many of the phenomena attributed to ESP in its various forms, from telepathy to psychometry, even clairvoyance and the ability to look into the future, can be explained without the need to assume a world beyond this one. Most of these ESP phenomena happen between living people, and although they may be in contravention of accepted laws of cause and effect, they nevertheless do not imply the existence of another order of things, one which necessitates a radical rethinking of one's philosophy. But when we come to the question of ESP communication with the realm of the dead, we are opening a Pandora's box. If there is such a thing as communication with the so-called dead, then our biological concept of life and man needs to be greatly modified. Nearly all "establishment" scientists, especially in medicine, postulate that the physical body of man is nearly all there is, with mind taking the role of a personality complex rather than an invisible unit. Until the discovery of psychiatry and, later, psychoanalysis, the concept of a mind separate from the body was as unacceptable to those scientists as the concept of another dimension beyond death is to them today.

Perhaps the strongest reason why the existence of a world of the dead is so difficult to accept by the scientifically minded lies in the seeming invisibility of that realm. Trained to accept only that which we can see, hear, touch, or otherwise come in direct contact with by our five senses, we find it difficult to give credence to a set of conditions that we cannot measure with those same senses. We are forced to go by assumptions, deduced by the testimony of others, and to work with indirect material rather than with the direct approach so useful in dealing with physical matters. But this is merely prejudice on our part. Many areas of human knowledge are based upon invisible values: We know that electricity and electric current can accomplish certain things and we can measure the results, but we cannot actually see the electric current flowing through a wire. Even if we touch the wire and receive a shock, we are merely experiencing the result rather than the causative element itself. To be able to photograph electricity, we have to conduct it through certain substances, such as gases, before we are able to trace, and thus photograph, it, but the current itself remains invisible without help. Magnetic waves cannot be seen by the naked eye nor can they be touched. They can, however, be measured by sensitive instruments and the result of magnetism is capable of verification. Perhaps an even better parallel lies in the causative factors of disease. Until man invented microscopes sensitive enough to see microbes, he did not know about them. He assumed that illnesses were caused by a variety of factors, ranging from ill will of the gods to human accidents.

Once we have perfected sensitive instruments to measure the etheric body in man, we will be able to understand its workings a great deal better. At the present time we can only assume that it exists because we see it at work in psychic phenomena. It seems, as the late Bishop James Pike might have put it, "the best of several possible alternatives." We have photographed the human aura, the electromagnetic field that reaches out beyond the human skin and indicates the state of health of the individual, among other things. We have measured and studied the tiny electrical currents going through the nerve fibers from the brain, and we know that the electro-encephalogram does not lie; electricity does go through the nerves. We can look at the heavens and see only a tiny portion of the bodies in space simply because our instruments are not refined enough to see it all. This does not mean that there do not exist additional worlds beyond those that we can currently register. It merely means that we have not yet been able to reach out that far. It is the same with "inner space": our inability to record objectively the very fine elements making up the etheric body within should in no way be confused with the absence of that body. Everything in the study of paranormal phenomena indicates the existence of such a body within man; taken as a whole, the phenomena generally associated with ESP cannot be explained better than by assuming that man has within himself at all times an inner layer or dimension that is capable of breaking through the time-space barrier and accomplishing seemingly paranormal phenomena. I say "seemingly," because they are in fact perfectly normal phenomena that become extraordinary only because of our lack of comprehension. In Procrustean fashion, we make the observed facts fit the established theory instead of building a theory upon existing facts. This cannot, of course, go on forever; the scientific establishment is bound to re-form itself when the pressure to do so becomes unbearable.

As a matter of fact, the haphazard and surprising way in which communications from the so-called dead occur to the living, the suddenness of apparitions, the voice in an empty room identified with a known dead individual, visits from long-dead relatives and friends, farewell greetings at the time of passing—all these phenomena, which are very common indeed, would not be so numerous if we the living were not continuously bombarded with a philosophy of living based upon false values and false information. Whether we are materialistically inclined or pay lip service to an established religion, even if we are devout religionists, our attitude toward the possibility of spirit communication is inevitably one of doubt, if not of fear. Only a small minority of people are prepared to consider such occurrences as natural and desirable. Perhaps, in a world where the question of channels between the physical world and the next dimension is no longer one of doubt but one of certainty, the need for the dead to manifest to the living as much as they do now will be no longer compelling.

As I have pointed out through many examples published in an earlier work entitled *Life After Death: The Challenge and the Evidence*, the majority of communications between the dead and the living is for the purpose of acquainting the living with the continuous existence of the dead in another dimension. Whether the dead person himself has lacked this understanding in his lifetime in the physical world and now wants to make amends for it, or whether the living person to whom the communication is directed is in that sore state of ignorance and therefore needs to be educated by the dead individual for the living person's own benefit, the fact is that there is a compelling desire on the part of many "dead" individuals to let those they have left behind in the physical world know about their own world, about the fact that they continue to live a useful and seemingly complete life. A comparatively small number of such cases is due to unfinished business during the earth life of the deceased.

Scientists unfamiliar with the material on this subject tend to shrug off the apparitions of the dead or vocal phenomena along those lines as hallucinations, putting the blame on the observer and suggesting that either the phenomenon did not take place at all or was due to emotional and psychological malfunction in the observer himself. While this may hold true in a small number of cases and may be, on the surface at least, a possible explanation in a number of other cases where there exists an element of mourning, it certainly does not hold true in cases of "surprise visits" by dead individuals to people who did not know they had passed on, or who did not know them at all and who had to ascertain afterward from independent sources the identity of the apparition they had seen. Such cases, in fact, are in the majority among those observed by sane, sound individuals and told to reliable witnesses or registered in the records of reputable research societies. People stay at houses and are surprised by the apparition of a dead individual about whom they know nothing. Later, on checking their experience, they find that they have seen a dead person formerly associated with the house. People are visited by strangers who represent themselves to them as long-dead relatives; on checking with family members, the identity is later established. People report the appearance of a dear one at the same time as the family member is dying or has died, without, of course, the knowledge of the time or place of death. All this is well established and documented in the files of such research societies as the American Society for Psychical Research, the British College of Psychic Sciences, or, for that matter, my own very extensive files. That there is another dimension close to this one in which we live I do not doubt in the least. The nature of that dimension seems essentially to be a thought world; everything consists of specific electromagnetic fields, containing memories and emotional stimuli identifiable with individuals formerly alive in physical bodies. For all practical purposes, then, the dead are nothing more than the inner selves of living people, looking like them, thinking like them, feeling like them, being able to move rapidly since they no longer have to carry the weight of a physical outer layer called a body.

The people who have had experiences of this kind with the "dead" run the gamut of professions, ages, national and educational backgrounds.

Mrs. Sally G. is a registered nurse in Georgia. "In the past I have worked with the National Institute of Health in Bethesda, Maryland," she explains. "I mention this because it was there in the Institute of Neurology that I was taught to note and describe full details. I am thirty-five years old and at the time of this incident I was living in the same town with my mother but my two children and I lived in a house that was several blocks away from my mother's house. My husband, Captain M.G., was at that time serving another tour in Vietnam. My brother, Captain Joseph D., was in Army Intelligence in Vietnam when on February 28, 1967, his plane crashed and burned. The pilot and my brother died instantly.

"Several months after my brother's death my mother fell and broke her hip and dislocated her shoulder. Naturally she had to be hospitalized, and when she returned home about a month later, she had to have around-the-clock help. When this incident I am about to relate occurred, she was not in the house alone but had a practical-duty night nurse who was then in the living room. My mother's apartment was on the downstairs floor. At the time she had her bedroom door closed and her room was definitely darkened as she had always been a light sleeper and was sensitive to noise and lights. She was lying in bed and was beginning to feel very relaxed, although she was not yet asleep, when the room suddenly seemed to be illuminated and sort of 'pressurized.' Then she saw her son, Joseph, standing near the foot of her bed, smiling at her. She could see him as clearly as if it were daylight."

There followed a brief conversation between mother and son, in the course of which she asked him how his father was and he replied that his father, who had passed away four years before, was fine. The vision then disappeared, but Mrs. D. could still sense him in the room with her. She began to tremble and started to cry. She called out to her night nurse, but since the door was closed the nurse couldn't hear her, so Mrs. D. picked up a small object from her night table and threw it against the door. The nurse, Mrs. F.S., came into the room, where Mrs. D. was now crying uncontrollably. When the nurse entered the room, Mrs. D. cried out, "Oh, Mrs. S., Joseph was here." To her surprise, the nurse replied, "Yes, I know. I saw a brown shadow go past the dining-room table."

The following morning Mrs. D. became somewhat calmer after she had informed her daughter of the event of the previous night. Another nurse was on duty then, and shortly after she had had her nursing care Mrs. D. went back to bed with the intention of taking a nap, since she had been awake so much of the previous night. As soon as she was alone in her room with the door shut, her dead son reappeared suddenly and said to her, "Mother, I am sorry that I frightened you last night." Then he disappeared again. This time, however, Mrs. D. was not upset. For one thing it convinced her that she had not been dreaming the incident the night before. There was no doubt about it; the apparition had been that of her late son, Joseph. He had appeared quite solid, not transparent, as legendary ghosts usually are. Mrs. D., under questioning by her daughter, Mrs. G., stated that Joseph had been dressed in civilian clothing, a shirt and pants. Mrs. G. thought that that was significant because her brother, Joseph, although an Army career man, had been bitter toward the service at the end and would have wanted to appear in civilian clothing on his last journey.

William Hull of Brooklyn, New York, is a member of an amateur theatrical group called the Promenade Players. Here is his statement dated August 17, 1970:

"During our last show, our director, Joan Bray, became quite ill, and, in fact, nearly died. Joan loves to entertain, especially us in the group, but because of her illness had not been able to most of the summer. On July 31 of this year she felt good enough to have us over for dinner. She invited half of the group on Friday and the rest for Monday, August 3. Because he had moved and not left a phone number, she had not been able to contact Chuck Taylor, our lead in the last show. While she was preparing dinner on Friday afternoon, the thirty-first, Chuck called and in a characteristic manner asked when he would be invited over for dinner. Joan told him he could come either that evening or the following Monday. He replied that he would much rather come when he could eat alone with Joan and her teen-age daughter. Joan didn't think this request out of the ordinary as Chuck was a person who was always 'on stage' with a group but liked to relax and was a different person when he was alone with someone. So no definite date was set, but Chuck did give Joan a phone number to reach him at so that she could invite him when she felt like it. Then, in closing the telephone conversation, Chuck made an unusual request: 'Take care of yourself, Joan,' he said in a rather sober voice. Joan replied that of course she would. 'No, I really mean it. Take care of yourself,' he repeated. Again Joan replied that she always took care of herself. To placate him, Joan promised and this ended the conversation. Joan didn't think about the conversation except to mention to those of us that asked that she had heard from Chuck and he had left a number to reach him.

"About the twelfth of August a photographer friend of mine, also a member of our group, tried to contact Chuck to tell him that some long-ago ordered prints were finally ready. He discovered that Chuck had collapsed and died on the seventeenth of July. Of course, we thought that there must be some mistake, but by careful check we found that he had indeed died and had been buried on the twentieth. Now the only other explanation was that it was not Chuck that called that afternoon, but Joan Bray knew Chuck better than anyone else. Her long and close relationship with him seemed to rule out any possibility of an imposter calling."

Romer Troxell, forty-two-year-old father of twenty-four-year-old Charles Troxell, whose body had been found punctured with bullets and stripped of identification by a roadside in Portage, Pennsylvania, in 1970, can attest to the reality of communication from the dead. According to the United Press International, as published by the Los Angeles *Times* of May 30, 1970, the father kept hearing the son's voice directing him to the accused killer. It all started when he looked at the face of his dead son in the Portage morgue. "My son just simply spoke to me," the father is quoted as saying, "He said, 'Hi, pop. I knew you would come. He's got my car.'"

After the body had been positively identified, the father was notified. Since the police were tight-lipped about the investigation, Troxell and his family went to stay with his brother in Gary. But he became restless and found himself in his car with his wife and sister-in-law as if he were searching for something. His dead son, Charles, was guiding him. He drove along a road he had not been on before when he suddenly heard his dead son's voice telling him, "Here he comes, Pop." But there was just a hill ahead and no sign of any car. Then he saw the yellow Corvette coming over the crest and Charlie told him, "Here he comes, Pop. Take it easy. He is armed. Don't get excited. He's going to park soon." The father followed the car, and as soon as it had parked outside a high school he went up to the young driver later identified as the murderer. "The boy knew who I was," the father continued his story. "He said he had seen my car at my brother's home." But he claimed that Charles had sold him the car, adding that he had not seen Charles for two days. When the father asked, "Are you sure?" the boy said, "No, but isn't he dead?" Then Mr. Troxell knew he had the killer before him because his son's identity had not been published in the newspapers and only the police and the family knew about it. As the father continued his conversation with the young man, he again heard his son's voice saying, "Be careful, Pop. He's got a gun." Under the circumstances, Mr. Troxell decided to play it lightly. He knew that the police, summoned by his sister-in-law, were en route. As soon as the boy had been arrested and charged with the murder, the son's spirit voice faded and has not been back since.

Examples like these can be found by the thousands, all fully documented. Communications between the living and the dead, whether initiated by the dead or by the living, use the faculty of ESP to make themselves felt. Only if the recipient of such communication has sufficient ESP to convert the very fine emanations sent out from the nonphysical world can the conscious mind register the information. An emergency, an emotional necessity, or any kind of urgency will make the impact much stronger of course. In the cases just discussed, the need to communicate was present. Ordinary communication was impossible. The majority of such ESP communications from the dimension beyond the physical are initiated by the dead themselves. All the recipient can hope for is to be a good channel. The way to accomplish this is to achieve a relaxed attitude of body, mind, and spirit; by relaxing the body, the nervous system is likely to exclude external interference and disturbances; the mind, by clearing itself of cross current thoughts and becoming as much of a blank as possible, permits itself to serve as a receiver; and the spiritual self, by accepting the reality of such communications and the higher guidance that it implies, ties it all up in a neat package of possible breakthroughs.

To initiate communication with the dead via the ESP route is another matter. If there were a compelling reason for such communication, putting oneself in a state of receptiveness would, of course, be the first step. Visualizing the desired contact on the "other side" of life may help if a specific contact is desired. But you cannot summon the dead; you cannot reach out to them at will and command them to appear or get in touch with you. At the very best, you can hope to set up conditions favorable to their wanting to communicate with you. If your need is genuine and your state is one of relaxed receptiveness, then the communication may very well occur. Patience and a certain disregard of time is also valuable, since conditions may appear favorable to us but are in fact not so when seen from the point of view of the "other side."

At any rate, there is no other way of communicating with the nonphysical world except by ESP. Only thought forms can break through the barrier separating the two worlds. The stronger your ESP, the more disciplined your application of it, the more likely it is that you will be able to have contact with those who have gone on to the nonphysical world.

CHAPTER VII

ASTRAL PROJECTION, BILOCATION, AND ESP

One of the terms frequently met with in the discussions
of paranormal phenomena is the word "astral." Although
vaguely reminiscent of stars and celestial conditions, it
actually means the same as etheric, at least to me it does.
By astral or etheric dimension, I mean that world outside
the physical world which contains all spiritual phenomena
and ESP manifestations. This dimension is made up of
very fine particles and is certainly not intangible. The
inner body, which in my opinion represents the true personality in man, is made up of the same type of substance; consequently, it is able to exist freely in the astral
or etheric dimension upon dissolution of the physical
body at physical death. According to theosophy and, to a
lesser degree, the ancient Egyptian religion, man has five
bodies of which the astral body is but one, the astral
world being the second lowest of seven worlds, characterized by emotions, desires, and passions. This, of course, is
a philosophical concept. It is as valid or invalid as one
chooses it to be. By relating to the astral world as merely
the "other side of life," I may be simplifying things and
perhaps run counter to certain philosophical assumptions,
but it appears to me that to prove one nonphysical sphere
is enough at this state of the game in parapsychology. If

there be other, finer layers—and I do not doubt in the least that there are—let that be the task at a time when the existence of the nonphysical world is no longer being doubted by the majority of scientists.

In speaking of "astral projection," we are in fact speaking of projection into the astral world; what is projected seems to be the inner layer of the body, referred to as the astral or etheric body. By projecting it outward into the world outside the physical body, it is capable of a degree of freedom that it does not enjoy while encased in the physical body. As long as the person is alive in the physical world, however, the astral body remains attached to the physical counterpart by a thin connecting link called the "silver cord." If the cord is severed, death results. At the time of physical death, the cord is indeed severed and the astral body freely floats upward into the next dimension. Nowadays we tend to call such projections "out-of-the-body experiences." Robert Monroe, a communications engineer by profession and a medium by accident, has written a knowledgeable book about his own experiences with out-of-the-body sensations, and a few years before him, Dr. Hereward Carrington, together with Sylvan Muldoon, authored a book, considered a classic nowadays, on the subject of astral projection. The reason that out-of-the-body experience is a more accurate term to describe the phenomena is to be found in the fact that projection, that is to say a willful outward movement out of the physical body, is rarely the method by which the phenomena occur. Rather it is a sensation of dissociation between physical and etheric body, a floating sensation during which the inner self seems to be leaving its physical counterpart and traveling away from it. The movement toward the outside is by no means rapid or projectionlike; it is a slow gradual disengagement most of the time and with most witnesses. Occasionally there are dramatic instances where astral projection occurs spontaneously and rather suddenly. But in such cases some form of shock or artificial trauma is usually present such as during surgery and the use of an anesthetizing agent or in cases of sudden grief, sudden joy, or states of great fatigue.

Out-of-the-body experiences can be classified roughly into two main categories: the spontaneous cases, where it occurs without being induced in any way and is usually as a surprise, and experimental cases, where the state of dissociation is deliberately induced by various means. In the latter category certain controlled experiments are of course possible, and I will go into this toward the end of this chapter.

The crux of all astral projection, whether involuntary or voluntary, is the question whether the traveler makes an impact on the other end of the line, so to speak. If the travel is observed, preferably in some detail, by the recipient of the projection, and if that information is obtained after the event itself, it constitutes a valuable piece of evidence for the reality of this particular ESP phenomenon.

There is the case of a Japanese–American lady, Mrs. Y., who lived in New York and had a sister in California. One day she found herself projected through space from her New York home to her sister's place on the West Coast. She had not been there for many years and had no

idea what it looked like inasmuch as her sister had informed her that considerable alterations had taken place
about the house. As she swooped down onto her sister's
home, Mrs. Y. noticed the changes in the house and saw
her sister, wearing a green dress, standing on the front
lawn. She tried to attract her sister's attention but was
unable to do so. Worried about her unusual state of being,
that is, floating above the ground and seemingly being
unable to be observed, Mrs. Y. became anxious. That
moment she found herself yanked back to her New York
home and bed. As she returned to her own body, she experienced a sensation of falling from great heights. This
sensation accompanies most, if not all, incidents of astral
travel. The feeling of spinning down from great heights is,
however, a reverse reaction to the slowing down in speed
of the etheric body as it reaches the physical body and
prepares to return into it. Many people complain of
dreams in which they fall from great heights only to
awaken to a sensation of a dizzying fall and resulting
anxiety. The majority of such experiences are due to astral
travel, with most of it not remembered. In the case of
Mrs. Y., however, all of it was remembered. The following
day she wrote her sister a letter, setting down what she
had seen and asking her to confirm or deny the details
of the house and of herself. To Mrs. Y.'s surprise, a letter
arrived from her sister a few days later confirming everything she had seen during her astral flight.

Ruth E. Knuths, a former schoolteacher who currently
works as a legal secretary in California, has had many
ESP experiences, and like many others, she filed a report
in conformity with a suggestion made by me in an earlier

book concerning any ESP experiences people wished to register with me.

"In the spring of 1941 when I lived in San Diego, where I had moved from Del Rio, Texas, I was riding to work on a streetcar. I had nothing on my mind in particular; I was not thinking of my friends in Texas and the time was 8:00 A.M. Suddenly I found myself standing on the front porch of Jo Comstock's house in Del Rio. Jo and I have been friends for many years. The same dusty green mesquite and cat claw covered the vacant lot across the road, which we called Caliche Flat. People were driving up and parking their cars at the edge of the unfenced yard. They were coming to express sympathy to Jo because of the death of her mother. Jo was inside the house. I knew this although I did not see her. I was greeting the friends for her. The funeral was to be that afternoon. Then as suddenly as I had gone to Del Rio, I was back in the streetcar, still two or three blocks away from my stop.

"Two weeks later Joe wrote, telling me that on a certain date, which was the same date I had this vision on, her mother had been found by neighbors unconscious from a stroke, which they estimated had occurred about ten o'clock in the morning. Jo was notified at 10:30. She said that she badly wished me to be there with her. Allowing for the difference in time, two hours, I had had this experience at the time of the stroke, but the vision itself was projected ahead of that two days, to the day of the funeral."

On May 28, 1955, she had another experience of astral projection, which she was able to note in detail and report to me:

"My husband and I had dinner with Velva and Jess

McDougle and I had seen Jess one time downtown, afterward, and we spoke and passed. I had not seen Velva.
Then on June 11, a Saturday, I was cleaning house,
monotonously pushing the vacuum sweeper brush under
the dresser in the bedroom, when suddenly I was standing
at the door of a hospital room, looking in. To the left,
white curtains blew gently from a breeze coming from a
window. The room was bright with sunlight; directly op-
posite the door and in front of me was a bed with a man
propped up on pillows; on the left side of the bed stood
Velva. The man was Jess. No word was spoken, but I knew
that Jess was dead, although as I saw him he was alive
though ill. I 'came back' and was still cleaning under the
dresser. I didn't contact Velva, nor did I hear from her.
However, about a week later my sister, Mary Hatfield,
told me that she was shocked to hear of Mr. McDougle's
death. That was the first confirmation I had. I immediately went to see Velva, and she told me that he had
suffered a heart attack on Thursday before the Saturday
of my vision, and had died the following Sunday, the day
after the vision occurred."

Richard Smith is a self-employed landscape service con-
tractor, in his thirties, married and living in Georgia. He
has had many ESP experiences involving both living
people and the dead. Sometimes he is not sure whether he
has visions of events at a distance or is actually traveling
to them. In his report to me he states:
"On one very unusual occasion, just before sleep came,
I found myself floating through the air across the country
to my wife's parents' home in Michigan where I moved
about the house. I saw Karen's father as he read the news-

paper, his movements through the rooms, and drinking a cup of coffee. I could not find her mother in the house. She was apparently working at the hospital. I was floating at a point near the ceiling and looking down. Mr. Voelker, her father, happened to look up from his coffee and seemed to be frightened. He looked all around the room in a state of great uneasiness as if he could sense me in the room. He would look up toward me but his eyes would pass by as though I were invisible. I left him, as I did not wish to frighten him by my presence.

"This latter experience I seem almost able to do at will when the conditions are right, and travel anywheres. Sometimes, involuntarily, I find myself looking upon a scene that is taking place miles away and of which I have no personal knowledge. These experiences have taken place since my childhood, although I have kept them to myself with the exception of my wife."

Astral travel is so common an experience that the files of the American Society for Psychical Research are bulging with this type of report. The loosening of the bonds between conscious and unconscious mind can be due to a number of factors, chiefly a state of relaxation just before the onset of sleep or just before awakening. It would appear that the physical body and the inner, etheric body are not as solidly intertwined in everyone as one might be led to believe. When thoughts wander and a person's attention drifts, the inner body containing the true personality may slip out involuntarily, accidentally as it were, and wander about, leading a life of its own unencumbered by the controlling influence of the conscious mind. It may be attracted to strange scenes or it might find itself compelled to well-known places or persons. The material on hand in research institutions seems to indicate a wide variety of goals.

Induced astral projection has been a subject that has fascinated physical researchers almost from the start of modern parapsychology. Because such experiments are repeatable and offer satisfactory control conditions, they are frequently used to demonstrate the presence of ESP capabilities in people. Certainly astral projection is more capable of being artificially induced than any other form of ESP. It is the one form of ESP that does not require true emotional motivation to succeed. The adventure and excitement of leaving one's body, even if temporarily, seems to be sufficient to stimulate the apparatus capable of producing the phenomenon.

Some fifteen years ago, when I was working with a group of interested students headquartered at the New York City offices of the Association for Research and Enlightenment, better known as the Cayce Foundation, we had at our disposal a young man named Stanley G. who was capable of deliberate astral projection. One experiment consisted of setting up controlled conditions in an apartment on East Eighty-second Street while another team met at the A.R.E. headquarters on West Sixteenth Street. The team on Eighty-second Street was free to choose certain control conditions and decided to use as their earmarks an open book, marked at a certain page and at a certain line on that page, plus a flower in a vase Stanley was placed into light hypnotic trance in the office on West Sixteenth Street and was directed to visit the Eighty-second Street place, to report back after awakening everything he had observed, and, if possible, to make his presence known to the observers on the other end. The entire experiment took no more than half an hour. When it was completed, Stanley woke up, rubbed his eyes, and started to report what he had experienced. Apparently, shortly after he had projected himself outward from his physical body, he had found himself floating through the apartment on Eighty-second Street. He remarked that he went to the kitchen of the apartment, which he found bathed in blue-white light. At all times he had the sensation of being slightly above the floor, floating rather than actually walking upon it. He clearly saw the observers and, upon awakening, described them to the team on West Sixteenth Street. He also described the flower in the vase and the book that had been opened to a certain page. However, he could not arouse the observers to acknowledge his presence, even though he tried to touch them. His hand seemed to go right through them, and he was unable to make his presence known to them.

Controlled astral projection should not be undertaken by anyone without a helper standing by to arouse him if necessary; for instance, if should there be any difficulties in his coming back to his own body. This is not to say that such projection may be dangerous, despite the dire warnings sounded by certain occultists. I know of no single incident where evil entities have taken advantage of the situation and "slipped into" the body of an astral traveler while the owner was out. The danger, if any, of unobserved and uncontrolled astral travels lies in the lack of control of the time element, and the inability of the traveler to report immediately upon awakening what he might have encountered. It is therefore best to have another person standing by from beginning to end of the experiment.

People with somnambulistic tendencies are most likely to succeed in exteriorizing the astral body. These are people with mediumistic tendencies, very imaginative and very easily influenced. Hardheaded, businesslike, or basically suspicious individuals make poor astral travelers. This is not to say that imagination is necessary for out-of-the-body experiences to succeed. Nor should one assume that imaginary experiences are at the base of astral travel. Far from it; the experiences are quite real in every sense of the word. But it is true that the tendency toward imagery, a tendency toward dreaming, perhaps, is helpful to permit the purely mechanical disengagement of the astral body from its physical counterpart.

Thus whether the subject is particularly suitable to astral travel by his or her nature, or simply desirous of succeeding even though not particularly suited for it, the technique remains the same. It is best at an hour of the day when one is reasonably relaxed, possibly physically tired. The room in which the experiment is to take place must be quiet, not too brightly lit, and not too warm or too cold. Above all, there should be little noise or other distraction. The subject then stretches out on the couch or bed, closes his eyes, and pictures himself floating up from his body toward the ceiling. Inevitably, this self-suggestion leads to a sense of giddiness or lightheaded-ness. Eventually, the limbs will become lighter and may not be felt after a while. As the experiment is continued, the person will feel himself rise, or rather have a sensation of weightlessness. At this point it is possible that the disengagement from the physical body begins, and some

experimenters have described the sensation of slowly rising straight up to the ceiling of the room where they
would stop and look down upon their sleeping bodies.
Others have found themselves in the corner of the room,
somewhat frightened by it all, looking back upon their
sleeping counterparts. At all times, the personality and
the seat of the ego remain in the astral body. The sleeping
physical body continues to breathe regularly and maintain
its functions as if the personality of the astral traveler
were still inside it. This is made possible by the connecting silver cord, which serves as a link between the two
bodies, a kind of cable through which impulses go back
and forth.

It is important to realize that the moment of disengagement is by no means a moment of panic or confusion: the
astral traveler thinks clearly, perhaps more clearly than
when he is in the physical body. He is capable of directing himself toward whatever goal he has chosen. He may,
at his discretion, choose to wander about or simply
float out the window without any particular aim in mind,
but he will be able to observe quite clearly the world
around him. In this state the astral traveler is able to
partake of two worlds: the physical world, which he has
just left temporarily, and the nonphysical world, in which
the so-called dead lead their continued existence. Thus it
may well be that the astral traveler will find himself face
to face with friends or relatives who have passed on or
with people who are strangers yet seem quite clearly no
longer in the physical life. From the astral traveler's point
of view, there is no difference between the so-called dead
individuals he encounters in flight and the living people

he sees. Both seem three dimensional to him and there is no feeling of transparency or two-dimensional appearance. There is also a total absence of the sense of time. Consequently, the traveler may not realize how long he has been out of the body. He is, however, capable of ending his excursion at will. If this happens with a sense of panic, the return trip will be a rough one and the awakening in the body may be accompanied by headaches and possibly nausea. Consequently, out-of-the-body travelers who experiment with this state of consciousness should not allow themselves to be drawn back too quickly; they should slowly direct themselves back toward their homes, suggesting that they descend slowly and without undue haste until they find themselves once again in familiar surroundings. When they arrive above their physical bodies, hovering above them for a moment, as it were, they will then direct themselves to descend the rest of the way until they "click" into place inside their physical bodies. This clicking into place is an important part of the return. The sensation of clicking into place has been described by nearly all astral travelers. If it does not occur, there may be delayed reactions upon awakening, such as a sense of displacement, confusion, or a dual presence. If this has happened, the subject must be hypnotized, and during hypnosis full reintegration of the astral and physical bodies is suggested; then the subject is brought out of hypnosis and the integration will have taken place. This, however, is rarely necessary. Since astral travel requires a fair degree of energy, and since this energy comes from the physical body of the subject, the traveler should rest immediately following his return and partake of some liquids to replenish his supply, which will definitely have been reduced during the out-of-the-body experience.

The majority of out-of-the-body experiences take place during sleep, and form one of the four types of "dream states" described by individuals upon awakening. The other three are dreams due to physical discomfort, dreams due to suppressed material that is of significance to psychoanalysts and psychotherapists, and precognitive dreams, in which future events are foreseen. The difference between an out-of-the-body experience during sleep and ordinary dreams is quite marked. Ordinary dreams are frequently remembered only in part, if at all, and are quickly forgotten even if they are remembered upon awakening; astral projections are remembered clearly and in every detail, and seemingly last several days in one's memory. They compare to other dreams the way a color photograph compares to a black and white print. It stands to reason that the majority of out-of-the-body experiences occur during sleep, when the bonds between conscious and unconscious minds are relaxed. Occasionally, people have out-of-the-body experiences while fully awake, not only when resting or sitting down, but even while driving cars or walking. Some of these experiences are of very short duration, and I know of no instance where accidents have occurred due to this momentary displacement. There seems to be some sort of superior law watching over individuals with this particular gift, making sure that they do not suffer because of it. In the case of motorists driving along a highway at great speed and having momentary displacements, this seems particularly likely, since any purely logical explanation would simply not account for the amazing fact that accidents do not occur under such circumstances.

I know of no other field of scientific inquiry where so little progress is apparent on the surface than in parapsychology. I do not mean to say that progress is not being made—far from it—but in terms of public knowledge very little is being disclosed that hasn't already been disclosed ten or fifteen years ago. Perhaps this may be due to the fact that the climate for disclosures of this kind was more favorable in the 1950s and early sixties than it seems to be today. Funds were available then that are not now at hand, but beyond this I notice a timidity on the part of responsible scientists in the field of parapsychology for which there is neither need nor explanation; the material obtained through the proper observation of spontaneous phenomena in ESP is tremendous and deserves a wider circulation, even in the popular sense of the term. On the other hand, material published ten or fifteen years ago is as valid today as it was when it was first disclosed to the public. Repeated experiments confirmed earlier findings and have continued to confirm them ad infinitum. As a matter of fact, it appears to me that some of these repeated experiments are no longer necessary since the point has long been made, and can be found in reputable published sources. The energies and funds used to prove those points over and over again could be better employed for research in areas where we do not yet have full confirmation of assumed facts.

What recent works on out-of-the-body experiences have said has already been said ably, if perhaps not as entertainingly, by the late Professor Hornell Hart, chairman of

the Committee on Spontaneous Cases, American Society
for Psychical Research, one-time associate professor at
Duke University, and a close collaborator of Professor
Rhine. Professor Hart, whom I recall as an amiable,
open-minded gentleman, is best remembered, to my mind
at least, as the scientist who said, after investigating numerous cases of so-called apparitions of the dead, "These
apparitions seem to be what they claim to be, namely, the
apparitions of the dead." On November 4, 1953, Professor
Hart submitted a summation of his intensive research into
out-of-the-body experiences. Entitled "ESP Projection:
Spontaneous Cases and Repeatable Experiments," the report covered a total of 288 cases of purported ESP projections and found that only ninety-nine of the 288 cases
investigated were evidential in terms of the project. These
ninety-nine cases were then classified into five types.
Three of these types involved purported ESP projections
produced experimentally: (a) the hypnotically induced
projections, which totaled twenty cases; (b) the projection of one's own apparition, by concentration, reported
in fifteen cases, and (c) self-projections by more elaborate
methods in twelve cases. Professional mediums, preliterate
medicine men, and amateur experimenters each have had
their own methods. The two types of spontaneous ESP
projections consisted of: (a) spontaneous apparitions of
the living, corresponding with dreams or other concentrations of attention by the appearers reported in thirty
cases, and (b) other spontaneous cases listed. Professor
Hart states, "The fifteen reported successes in projecting
one's own apparition plus the thirty spontaneous cases of
apparitions of living persons coinciding with dreams or

other directions of attention by the appearer suggest that such experiments are at least occasionally repeatable."

One of the arguments sometimes put forth by both parapsychologists and outsiders against the reality of astral travel involves the explanation of the phenomena as simple telepathy, clairvoyance, or precognition. In this respect Professor Hart makes the following observation: "(a) ESP projection does involve telepathy, clairvoyance, and precognition, (b) but simple telepathy and clairvoyance do not require projection of viewpoint; (c) ESP projection does involve perceiving from and being perceived in positions outside of the excursionist's physical body; (d) shared dreams involve ESP projection; (e) the ESP projection hypothesis provides a framework into which each of the ninety-nine evidential cases fits."

Professor Hart then concludes that the best method likely to produce full and verifiable ESP projections experimentally is hypnosis: "The suggestions given the hypnotized subject should make use of knowledge which has been accumulated relative to the basic characteristics of ESP projection as most fully experienced in the best cases reported to date. The induction of catalepsy, and suggestions that the astral body in being detached from the physical body, is floating upwards, is being lifted by unseen hands, and the like, should be promising in this connection. Responses should be elicited from the entranced individual to determine how far these subjected experiences are being realized. Subsequent stages in typical ESP projection should then be suggested, such as the movement of the projected body into the vertical position, its movement to a position standing on the floor, its release from catalepsy, its projection through an open door into an adjoining room, going through a closed door or solid wall, projection to distant locations, with observations of people, objects and events at those locations, and the like, should follow."

Professor Hart acknowledges the possibility that astral travelers might encounter the spirits of the dead en route. "In view of the frequency with which contact with what appeared to be projected personalities of deceased persons has been reported in past cases, it is of major importance that this phase of ESP projection shall be explored open-mindedly."

He goes on to suggest that "if and when successful hypnotic projections have been established, experiments should be carried out with a view to transferring to the hypnotized subject the initiative in such projections and the capacity to induce them at will or under specified conditions."

Professor Hart's one-line summary of cases he has investigated contained such startling statements as, "announced experiment first to SPR; then succeeded" or "wrote plan to appear to mother; independent confirmation"; "worried about father, deliberately projected to him"; and among cases involving self-projection by other methods than mere concentration, "during séance, projected to mine explosion eight miles away"; "projected medium located body of missing man." Among the one-line summaries of spontaneous apparitions of the living, Hart lists, "apparition of worried mother of dying woman seen by nurse"; "wife projected to husband at sea; seen by cabin mate also."

In his summation of the investigation, Professor Hart lists the following findings as due to the research undertaken: (a) out-of-the-body experiences are frequent; (b) such experiences may be veridical; (c) ESP projections are reported evidentially to have been produced experimentally at least forty-seven times. Pilot studies at Duke University showed that, in representative samples of students, shared dreams were reported by 24 per cent; precognitive dreams by 36 per cent; perception of apparitions by about 10 per cent, and out-of-the-body experiences by 33 per cent.

Professor Hart then sums up the findings presented by the chairman at the International Conference of Parapsychological Studies at the University of Utrecht, the Netherlands, on August 3, 1953. These findings parallel his own findings based largely upon experiments at Duke University and the careful re-evaluation of reported spontaneous cases.

Bilocation is a phenomenon closely allied with astral travel, but it is a manifestation of its own with certain distinct features that set it apart from astral travel or out-of-the-body experiences per se. In bilocation a living person is projected to another site and observed there by one or more witnesses while at the same time continuing to function fully and normally in the physical body at the original place. In this respect it differs greatly from astral projection since the astral traveler cannot be seen in two places at once, especially as the physical body of the astral traveler usually rests in bed, or, if it concerns a daytime projection, is continuing to do whatever the person is doing rather automatically and without consciousness. With bilocation there is full consciousness and unawareness that one is in fact being seen at a distance as well.

Bilocation occurs mostly in mentally active people, people whose minds are filled with a variety of ideas, perhaps to the point of distraction. They may be doing one thing while thinking of another. That is not to say that people without imagination cannot be seen at two places at once, but the majority of cases known to me do indeed fall into the first category. A good case in point is a close friend of mine by the name of Mina Lauterer of California. I have written of her previously in *ESP and You.* Miss Lauterer has pronounced ESP talents. In addition, however, she is a well-balanced and very keen observer, since she is a professional writer. She has had several experiences of being seen in a distant place while not actually being there in the flesh.

In one such case she was walking down the street in Greenwich Village, New York, when she saw a gentleman whom she knew from Chicago. Surprised to find this person out of his usual element, she crossed the street in order to greet him. She tried to reach out toward him and he evaporated before her eyes. The incident so disturbed her that she wrote to the man in Chicago and found out that he had been in Chicago at the time she had observed him in New York. However, he had just then been thinking of her. Whether his thought projection was seen by Mina Lauterer or whether a part of himself was actually projected to appear is a moot question. What is even more interesting is the fact that he, too, saw Miss Lauterer at the same time he was thinking about her in Chicago. This, of course, is a case of double bilocation, something that does not happen very often.

In another instance, Miss Lauterer reported a case to me that had overtones of precognition in addition to bilocation. "One night not long ago, in New York, as I was in bed, halfway between sleep and being fully awake," she said, "I saw a face as clearly as one sees a picture projected on a screen. I saw it with the mind's eye, for my eyes were closed. This was the first experience that I can recall, where I saw, in my mind, a face I had never seen before.

"About six weeks later, I received an invitation to go to Colombia, South America. I stayed on a banana plantation in Turbo, which is a primitive little town on the Gulf of Urabá. Most of the people who live there are the descendants of runaway slaves and Indian tribes. Transportation is by launch or canoe from the mainland to the tiny cluster of nearby islands. The plantation was located near the airport on the mainland, as was the customs office. The village of Turbo is on a peninsula.

"One Sunday afternoon I went into town with my host, an American, and my Colombian friend. As we walked through the dirty streets bordered with sewage drains and looked around at the tin-roofed hovels and the populace of the place, I thought, this is the edge of the world.

"Sunday seemed to be the market day; the streets were crowded with people mostly of two hues, black and red-skinned. As we passed a drugstore, walking single file, a tall, handsome, well-dressed young man caught my attention. He seemed as out of place as I and my companions did. He did not look at me, even as I passed directly in front of him. It struck me as strange. South American men always look at women in the most frank manner. Also, he looked familiar, and I realized that this was the face that I had seen in my mind, weeks before in New York!

"The following day we were invited to cocktails by our neighbor, the Captain of Customs. He told us that a young flyer arrived every month around the same time, stopped in Turbo overnight, and then continued on his regular route to other villages. He always bunked in with his soldiers, instead of staying at the filthy hotel in the village. He mentioned that the young man was the son of the governor of one of the Colombian states, and that he had just arrived from Cartagena, the main office of his small airline.

"He brought the young man out and introduced him to us. It was the young man that I had seen in the village! I asked him if he had really arrived Monday morning and he later proved beyond all doubt that he had not been in Turbo on Sunday afternoon when I saw him. He was dressed in the same clothes on Monday as those that I had seen him wearing on Sunday in my vision.

"I do not know why I saw him when he wasn't there. Later he asked me to marry him, but I did not.

"When I and my companions went to Cartagena later on we checked and again confirmed the facts—he was miles away when I had seen him!"

I am indebted to Herbert Schaefer of Savannah, Georgia, for the account of a case of bilocation that occurred some time ago to two elderly friends of his.

Carl Pfau was awakened one night by the feeling that he was not alone. Turning over in bed, he saw his good friend Morton Deutsch standing by his bedside. "How did you get in here?" he asked, since the door had been securely locked. Deutsch made no reply but merely smiled, then, turning, walked to the door, where he disappeared. On checking the matter, it was discovered that Mr. Deutsch had been sitting in a large comfortable chair at the time of his appearance at this friend's bedside and had just wondered how his friend Carl was doing. Suddenly he had felt himself lifted from the chair and to Carl's bedside. There was a distance of about two miles between their houses.

Bilocation cannot be artificially induced the way astral projection can, but if you are bent on being seen in two places at once, you may encourage the condition through certain steps. For one thing, being in a relaxed and comfortable position in a quiet place, whether indoors or outdoors, and allowing your thoughts to drift might induce the condition. The more you concentrate, the less likely it is to happen. It is very difficult to produce that certain state of dissociation that is conducive to bilocation experiences. The only thing I can suggest is that such a condition may occur if you set up the favorable conditions often enough. It should be remembered that the majority of bilocation incidents is not known to the projected individual until after it has occurred and been confirmed on the other end.

CHAPTER VIII

OUIJA BOARDS AND OTHER PSYCHIC TOOLS

Probably one of the most common questions asked of me is what I think of ouija boards. More people seem to be using them these days than ever before and their numbers definitely are far greater than the tarot card decks or crystal balls in use at the present time among occult aficionados. To begin with, a ouija board is nothing more than a flat piece of wood, whether square, rectangular, or circular, upon which the letters of the alphabet, numerals one to nine, and the words "yes," "no," and "maybe" have been written. In conjunction with the board, people use a pointer made from plastic materials or wood. The pointer is large enough to place two hands upon it. Some variations of this instrument have a pencil stuck through them. The planchette is an older version of the ouija board and was popular in the late nineteenth century. It, too, relies upon the movement of a pointer guided by at least one hand. The term "ouija" is nothing more than the combination of the words *oui* and *ja*, both meaning yes in French and German respectively, and it refers to the two prominent questions asked of the alleged operator of the board as to certain personal problems, yes or no. The board itself has no special properties whatsoever. Neither has the pointer. When one or more persons, preferably two, operate the pointer placed upon the board, electro-magnetic energies flow from the bodies of the users into the board itself. Not unlike the membrane of a telephone, the energy then produces certain results. It may be, as with table tipping, simply crackling sounds due to the static electrical energy present or, more frequently, it may move the pointer about the board. Those who scoff at all psychic communications hold that the pointer is being moved across the board by the hands of those who oper-ate the gadget. This is quite true—but the impetus for the movement may come from other sources.

It is my personal conviction that in the majority of cases the unconscious mind of the person operating the pointer is responsible for the information obtained from it. This does not make the operation fraudulent by any means, but it does make it a simple extension tool of natural ESP. In a small number of cases, however, ex-ternal entities seem to be working through the hands of those who operate the pointer. The proof lies in the in-formation obtained in these cases, which was found to be totally alien to the people working the board or to anyone else in the vicinity, was of such a precise nature that it could not be attributed to guesswork or coincidence, yet was independently verified afterward.

Sometimes people with genuine hauntings in their houses attempt to find out what the cause of the phe-nomena is. They purchase a ouija board and try to make contact with the "hung-up" entity in the house. This is not recommended simply because a ghost, if genuine, is in no position to correspond rationally with the owner of the house, especially as he may be in conflict with the owner. Frequently unintelligible material, even words without meaning, comes through the ouija board. Some people have attributed these utterances to so-called elementals or mentally incompetent spirits. More likely, however, they are attempts by the unconscious of the sitter to exteriorize some undeveloped ideas. It should be remembered that the unconscious mind is free of all logical constraint and is sometimes quite childish, even immoral, and capable of extemporizing material, even in invented languages. The ouija board has been used widely by people in need of personal guidance in lieu of consulting the nearest astrologer or fortuneteller. Again, if answers received through this means could be known to the person asking the questions or anyone else present at the time, we must attribute them to the "tapping of the unconscious" of the sitter or sitters. There is nothing wrong with that and information may be gleaned in this manner that is ordinarily hidden in the person or persons involved. In this way, the board certainly helps unlock deeply felt emotions or information.

But the ouija board is not a toy. I find the idea that this instrument is being sold in large quantities to children and young people, for that matter to older people as well, unhealthy and objectionable on several counts. I find it unhealthy because it suggests that communication with the dead is a nice game that should be played by everyone. I find it unacceptable because there are occasional incidents involving a ouija board that are filled with danger. Should an operator be capable of deep trance mediumship and not be aware of it, if he uses a ouija board he may very well trigger the latent mediumship in himself. As a result, unwanted entities may take over, and if the person involved is not familiar with the techniques of controlling such invasions, all kinds of psychotic states may result.

While this is a rare possibility, it has nevertheless occurred. I spent several years assisting a New York lady, the wife of a prominent publisher, who had used the ouija board as a lark while on vacation with relatives. More to please her aged aunt and companion than out of any belief that it would really work, my friend found herself taken over by an unscrupulous and evil entity. It turned out that she had somehow been contacted by the departed spirit of a murderer who had found an entry wedge at that time and at that place into the physical world through the mediumship of my friend. Because of this careless "parlor game," my friend was literally possessed by this and other entities drawn to her, and her involuntary mediumship continued for a long time after. As a matter of fact, there had been latent traces of alcoholism, which, together with the overpowering influences of negative personalities were too much for her frail personality. I cannot condone the indiscriminatory advertising of ouija boards without precautionary instructions, at the very least; in particular, I find it offensive when mentalists, that is to say, stage entertainers, advertise such devices as harmless, when in fact they may not be.

As for veridical material obtained through the use of the ouija board, this occurs occasionally, also, and would probably occur by any other means of mediumship as well. The board is merely one of several devices that induces this state of consciousness and should not be confused with any kind of channel or actual probing device. Several years ago I sat with medium Ethel Johnson Meyers on her insistence that we try our hands at a ouija board, which at that time I looked at with jaundiced eyes. During that particular session a personality claiming to be a deceased soldier who had parachuted to his death in the Philippines during World War II manifested itself and gave the name of his parents and the circumstances of his passing. To my surprise, I discovered that he had had parents where he had indicated and the communication was apparently genuine. This was the more surprising as neither Mrs. Meyers nor I had any knowledge of this person beforehand and there seemed to be no particular significance for his "coming through" to us except that we had opened a channel of communication for him.

John H. Steinmeyer, Jr., is an underwriter for a large life insurance company, holds a Bachelor of Science degree in economics and sociology, with a minor in chemistry and biology, and has spent many years selling scientific apparatus to university medical research laboratories. In his early forties, he is married and has four children, making his home in one of the southern states. He has had a marked interest in parapsychology for at least fifteen years and might have followed it professionally if he had had the chance. Among other experimental attempts, he has devoted many hours to the ouija board, together with his wife and other combinations of approximately thirty persons during one year. Significant results were obtained, however, only when his wife and he operated the board together. He submits a particularly interesting example in his report to me:

"My cousin Harry Classen, whom I rarely see since he lives in Atlanta, stopped in to see us several months ago.

My wife and I were working the ouija board when he arrived with his wife. We knew only that he had been to Beaufort, South Carolina, that day. We continued with the ouija board and shortly afterward received a message for 'Harry' from Fred. We assumed that this referred to Harry's stepfather, Fred Huddelmeier, deceased two years ago. There were eight people in the room at the time and a third party took notes of what came through the board now. The first four lines were random words without significance, followed by just groups of letters, but then the name Jack was repeated several times. Following it came a word spelled differently several times although similar, something like 'polotic.' At the time I felt the board was attempting to write 'political' and I felt a slightly conscious effort on my part to help it spell correctly. Then the word 'land' repeated itself several times, followed by 'a land Edith asked about lies between a jambled marsh estate. Jack is crooked. Edith finds a happy life here.'

"Following the above message we asked Harry if it made any sense to him at all. He was obviously disturbed and told us he had gone to Beaufort for the sole purpose of settling some legal matters relating to property his mother, Edith, deceased about six months, had left at the time of her death. The realtor had a similar sounding name. Neither my wife nor I had ever heard the name. Also, significant to Harry was the fact that he vividly recalled that his stepfather, Fred, had disliked the man immensely and had on more than one occasion stated that he was 'dishonest.' To conclude, about a month later Harry told us that he had just been to Savannah to sign some legal papers connected with this property. In the interim, a title search had been required and they learned that an estate had once stood on part of this property, which is now covered by marshland. Harry had not known this at the time we received the message from Fred."

Lest there be any misgivings, the reference to the real estate man referred to the opinion of him is entirely that of the late Fred Huddelmeier, and not the author's, who has no opinion one way or the other.

Mr. Steinmeyer adds that the spelling in this particular message was very bad; for instance, the word "asked" was spelled "asced" and the real estate man's name was slightly misspelled. The communicator, the late Fred Huddelmeier, had been born and educated in Germany and had never attended an American school. Although deeply profound, he spoke with a decided accent, often used incorrect grammar, and probably spelled English poorly.

Mr. Steinmeyer then goes on to report another veridical experience with the ouija board.

"About eight months ago my wife and I were working the ouija board with approximately fifteen persons present. Among them were two young Marines visiting from Parris Island. We had met them only a short time before and knew nothing of their personal lives. A message came through for 'Bob.' We knew both were named Bob so I asked for a last name. It spelled 'Bearce.' I asked who the message was from and the board spelled 'Frances.' I asked Bob if he knew anyone named Frances and he replied that he did, so I quickly cautioned him not to say anything else that could possibly influence the message. We then asked for the message. It replied, 'Be a good boy.' Because I am basically a doubter, I asked Frances if she could tell us something neither I nor my wife could possibly know. 'She' replied with the word 'escort.' This made little sense so I asked, 'Escort where?' The reply was 'home.' I asked, 'Home from where?' Reply, 'California.' I then asked, 'When?' The reply was, '1955.' At this point we all noticed that Bob was visibly shaken. He had never seen a ouija board in his life, knew nothing about it, and obviously knew we knew nothing of what it said. He actually appeared near fainting, so I stopped and asked if he could explain. In 1954 he was a child of about ten years when he moved from Pennsylvania to California. He had an aunt named Frances, who was now deceased. In 1955 she escorted him on a trip from California back to Pennsylvania. Bob said he had certainly not been thinking about any of this at the time we got the message."

Now a very critical observer might think that this material, although entirely correct and of a very privy nature, could nevertheless have been drawn from the unconscious mind of Bob, since he knew of an aunt named Frances and the circumstances that were described in the message. This would presuppose that a ouija board can draw upon past memories no matter how hidden in a person's unconscious mind and bring them to the surface at will. It would also assume that the sitter's personality could detach part of itself to operate the ouija board and, as it were, reply to its own questions. All this is theoretically possible, but not very likely. In the view of the late Bishop James Pike, a good scientist must always take the most plausible hypothesis if there are several presented. But so long as material obtained through a ouija board or similar device is known to anyone present in the room, whether consciously or unconsciously, whether of current interest or totally forgotten, that shadow of a doubt must remain. Only when something is communicated through the ouija board that is totally unknown to all present and is checked out and found to be correct, or if a statement is made that becomes objective reality only after the session has ended, can we be completely sure that a genuine communication between a discarnate personality and living people has taken place.

Mr. Steinmeyer evidently had strong leanings toward absolute proof in science. He, too, demanded some sort of evidence that the material couldn't have been drawn from the unconscious of those present. Of the considerable volume of messages received by him and his group, ten messages were considered to have significance in an evidential way. A communicator calling himself "Sir Thomas Richards" gave them a message almost every time they had a session. One day in the summer of 1968, the communicator was asked to give some sort of proof that he was not just part of the unconscious of the six or seven people present but a real, separate entity. He replied immediately, saying that there would soon be great floods that would send thousands of people fleeing. Not satisfied with such a statement, Mr. Steinmeyer demanded to know where. The communicator replied, "Texas." About two weeks later a hurricane hit Texas and sent thousands fleeing, just as forecast by the entity on the ouija board.

Mr. Steinmeyer states, "Certainly I am not psychic in the sense of the persons about whom you write, but it is significant to me that on numerous occasions during the past ten years when I followed a strong hunch, almost a compulsion at times, to call on an account not on my original itinerary, I found that it was the most important call of the day or perhaps day of the year and that I could not have made the call on a more appropriate day. I was top man in a sales force of over sixty professional salesmen, and have often felt any success I had was due to feelings such as the foregoing, and the fortunate consequences of such insights, which were seemingly beyond my natural abilities at times."

Mrs. D. Thompson of Missouri has had ESP experiences of various kinds all her life. In 1966 her father suffered a severe heart attack and had to be hospitalized. During one of the occasions when she kept her father company in the hospital, Mrs. Thompson had a flash vision of a funeral scene in a cemetery and she knew then that it was her father's funeral she was seeing. Although this filled her with anxiety, her father recovered, and the following summer when the family met again, her vision had been all but forgotten. To while away the time, the brothers and sisters of the family decided to play with a ouija board and the board came up with some pretty weird things that shook them up somewhat; in particular, Mrs. Thompson recalled, when the board was asked where her father had been born. At the time of this question, the father was not in the house. To everyone's surprise, the communicator working the board replied, "Pineyville." They all laughed because they knew very well that he had been born in Doe Run. When her father returned home, she asked him about it and to her amazement he became very angry and told her to put the "damn fool thing" away.

But the funeral scene she had envisioned the year before came to pass. The day she and her brothers and sisters were coming home from the cemetery after burying their father, someone mentioned the incident with the ouija board and how strange it was that the communicator mentioned the wrong birthplace for her father. At this, an aunt of Mrs. Thompson's, an elder sister of her father's, spoke up saying that shortly after he had been born the area was incorporated into the town of Doe Run. However, it had been unofficially called "Pineyville" by residents. Since Mrs. Thompson's father had not been present during the particular ouija board session when the information about Pineyville came through the board, and since that information was totally unknown to all those present at the time, there remains the inescapable conclusion that this information was communicated to them from an outside source working the ouija board, not from any of the unconscious minds of those present.

Those who wish to use ouija boards may, of course, do so, as long as they realize that the boards represent a certain degree of danger to those unfamiliar with the possibilities, especially to those latent deep trance mediums who do not realize their gift. However, a well-read person in the psychic field, familiar with the various phases of ESP, should have no difficulty using the board without undue risks. Although, in order to exclude self-delusion, it is wise to look at any information obtained in this manner in the light of what has just been said. If any of the information is known to those present, it should not be regarded as fully evidential. Should, however, material be obtained that is unknown to all present and subsequently verified, then additional material could be taken with a degree of acceptance and the ouija board may then very well be an opening wedge for psychic communications.

As for the actual use of the board, it should be remembered that the hands of the operators do indeed move the indicator, the pointer, but do so allegedly under guidance from either the unconscious of the operators or an external source, possibly a spirit personality. It is therefore important to rest the hands as lightly as possible on the instrument, to exert no force whatsoever, and to learn to yield to even the slightest nudge received through one's nervous and muscular apparatus. It is helpful to exclude all conscious thoughts to the degree one is able to do so. Resting the fingertips rather than the entire palm of the hand on the instrument and yielding to even the slightest sense of movement will produce the best results. Under no circumstances should one push or move the indicator consciously or deliberately. Fraud in this case is pure self-delusion, not likely to yield any results at all.

Closely related to the ouija board is the talent known as "automatic writing." Here the person endeavoring communication with an external source allows the pen or pencil to be guided by that source. The hand holding the pen or pencil lightly on paper, ready to follow the slightest movement without resistance, is similar to the hand resting on the indicator on the ouija board. There is one marked difference between the two methods of communication, however, and that is the character of the handwriting, which may or may not be recognized as belonging to a deceased person. As a matter of fact, one of the evidential elements in automatic writing is recognition of the handwriting as belonging to another individual.

It is, of course, true that handwriting can be imitated, especially in a case where the alleged communicator is known to the automatic writer; knowledge of that person's handwriting is very likely to exist at least on the unconscious level. Nevertheless, graphologists and handwriting experts can usually tell whether a handwriting is a clever copy or the real thing, especially if sufficient samples are at hand. In addition to being guided, as it were, by an unseen hand, the automatic writer receives information and impulses to write down sentences faster than he ordinarily would be able to do. One of the earmarks of genuine automatic writing is the tremendous speed with which dictation takes place. But here, too, the proof of the pudding lies not only in the appearance of the writing, the lack of time to make up the sentences being written, but also in the nature of the information being transmitted. If any of it is known to the writer, whether consciously or unconsciously, it should be discounted as of evidential value. If, on the other hand, there are detailed and privy items of information contained in such scripts, then it is entirely possible that an authentic communication between a discarnate and a living person is taking place. Much rarer is automatic communication of this kind between two living individuals, but there are instances of that also on record. Just as with the ouija board, there are some inherent dangers in automatic writing. If the automatist is a deep trance medium and is not aware of that particular talent, unscrupulous entities may use the opening wedge of the automatic writing to enter the unconscious of the writer and possess him. Automatic writing is generally done alone. In most cases, illegible scribblings are the initial indication that an outside entity is about to possess the hand of the automatic writer. After a while the scribbled letters take on the shape of words, although many of the first words thus transmitted may be meaningless. Eventually, the sentences become more concise and the misspellings disappear unless, of course, misspelling was part of the character of the communicator.

Automatic writing has its place among genuine ESP communications. When it turns into a crutch upon which a person leans in order to avoid the realities of physical life, however, it loses its innocent aspects. In some cases, the automatic writer becomes a willing and totally uncritical instrument of the alleged communicator, submerging his own personality under the will of the automatic partner, doing his bidding, and living only for the next session with the unseen communicator. In other cases, automatic writing is followed by a more sophisticated form of communication, such as an apparition or an auditory phenomenon. As with ouija boards, the majority of automatic material can be explained on the basis of tapping the unconscious of the writer, but perhaps 20 per cent of the material scientifically evaluated by psychical research societies or parapsychologists such as myself seem to indicate a genuine communication with a deceased individual. The late New York columnist Danton Walker, a man with much ESP in his make-up but forever cautious about it, related to me his surprise when he received a compelling automatic communication from a man who claimed to have been killed during the Russian–Japanese War of 1905. The man identified himself as a Russian officer, gave his full name and other details that Danton Walker, with a newspaperman's nose for detail,

was able to verify. Why this Russian officer should pick
on Danton to tell his story, the late columnist never understood. Possibly it happened because Danton was the
only newspaperman around who was also mediumistic.
For anyone to be able to do automatic writing, or rather
to receive automatic writing, the person has to have a fair
degree of developed ESP. It is ESP that makes the communication possible, and that is what is at work in this unusual partnership between a living and a deceased individual.

Other tools useful with ESP communications include
such time-honored gadgets as the crystal ball, tarot
cards, coffee grounds, and tea leaves. All of them serve
merely as concentration points, and have no ESP qualities
of their own.

In the case of the crystal ball, the ability to focus one's
attention in a narrow channel and eventually perceive
visual imprints is called "scrying." Scrying is a talent some
individuals possess to the exclusion of all other ESP talents. Those easily given to vertigo or headaches should
not attempt it. The proverbial crystal ball, so dear to the
heart of newspaper cartoonists whenever they draw an alleged medium or gypsy fortuneteller, is actually nothing
more than a smooth piece of glass, or, in some cases, natural crystal, which captures a light beam in such a manner that it reduces the outside world to insignificance for
the observer. By thus eliminating external disturbances,
the scryer is able to tune in on his own unconscious mind
and obtain veridical material from it. Even the colloquial
expression that one's crystal ball may be cloudy, meaning
that one does not foresee the future, has a certain basis in

fact. Whenever the channel of communication is not open, the crystal will not divulge any information and the glass remains unimpressed. But we must remember that the vision does not actually exist in the crystal or on its glass surface, but is merely reflected by the unconscious mind of the scryer. Those who wish to try crystal ball gazing or scrying may do so by placing their crystal ball on a firm, preferably dark surface, ridding themselves of as many diverting objects as possible, and placing themselves in a receptive mood, preferably in a quiet and not too brightly lit room. Concentrating their gaze upon the surface of the crystal, they will eventually "see" scenes taking place upon the surface. This exercise should be undertaken daily but not for more than ten or fifteen minutes at any one time in order not to cause eyestrain or headaches. If the experimenter is capable of scrying, results should be otained within a week.

Tarot cards could be discussed for volumes at a time, so deep is the symbolic meaning of each and every card in the deck. Originally a medieval device to divine the future, the cards are based upon ancient designs, although there doesn't seem to be any record that the ancients actually used tarot cards as such. They are more definitely established as being in wide use in Europe from the early sixteenth century onward, although they may have been used in the Orient even before then. Basically, the tarot cards contain coded and pictorialized information about various aspects of human nature. A person consulting the tarot is in effect consulting his own unconscious. The cards merely allow him to follow certain guidelines in which he confides. There are various ways to consult the tarot, depending upon the number of cards used and the number or extent of the desired readings. Best known is the Scottish, or Tree of Life, method, so called from the origin and appearance of the layout. Professional tarot readers may spend up to an hour laying out various combinations of cards, asking the person to be read to shuffle them repeatedly and eventually to draw at random a set number of cards from the deck for the reader to interpret. By touching the deck of cards repeatedly, the person to be read gives the psychic reader a great deal of psychometric material as well as his personal selection of cards, which may or may not indicate a link with fate and karma in the way the subject selects his cards. More than anything else, it is the power of ESP in the psychic reader that permits him to speak freely about the subject, especially when the subject is unknown to him. The cards are secondary; in a way, they open up the flood gates of ESP within the reader because he so believes and because he is stimulated by the rich symbolism of the cards. I doubt very much that anyone without significant traces of ESP in his make-up can give a satisfactory tarot reading. Countless tarot decks have been sold as toys or as parlor games, but only those who have some ESP can use them to advantage. Anyone wishing to familiarize himself with the method of using the tarot cards should consult the books on the subject by Edward Waite or Eden Gray.

Coffee grounds and tea-leaf readings, so dear to the heart of gypsy fortunetellers, are similar to tarot readings in that the pattern into which coffee grounds fall or tea leaves organize themselves when the liquid has been drained stimulate certain reactions in the psychic reader. If the reader sees an image in the dregs, he does so in much the same manner as a subject will see various images in inkblots during a Rorschach test, a well-known standby of psychiatrists. There is nothing supernatural or even remotely psychic in either coffee grounds or tea leaves by themselves. The result of such readings depends entirely upon the reader, and if he derives much stimulation from looking at coffee grounds and tea leaves, he will be a satisfactory reader. Two or more people looking at the coffee grounds or tea leaves may get entirely different impressions from them because, objectively, the grounds and leaves do not take on the shape of anything pertaining to the future. It is all in the eye of the beholder.

It should therefore be remembered that ESP does not depend on any psychic tool or inducer; that it is an inherent part of a person's make-up and can be enhanced whether or not tools are being used. Some of the devices now being offered in the market or in popular magazines as being useful to develop ESP are nothing more than commercial ways of romanticizing a most interesting subject. Other than the ESP test kit now in use at the New York Institute of Technology, where I teach parapsychology, or similar kits or sets in use at Duke University, psychic tools, even sophisticated-looking tools, seem to have little value and should be treated more as objects of amusement.

Not exactly a psychic tool, but nevertheless highly useful in psychical research and the enhancement of ESP powers in people is an instrument not originally designed for that purpose. Dr. Douglas Baker, the eminent British surgeon and parapsychologist, a member of the Royal College of Surgeons, and a prolific writer on the subject of ESP, has developed a machine that creates magnetic fields along carefully programed lines. The instrument and biomagnetism itself are of value primarily in the treatment of certain diseases and they have been extremely successful over the past few years, even though they are still in the experimental stage. But I discovered, more or less by accident, that the application of Dr. Baker's biomagnetic machine also helped to increase ESP tendencies in some professional mediums I work with. I place the head of a sensitive into a square open-wire cage, that is to say, a wooden box around which many layers of coated wire have been strung and through which a low intensity electromagnetic current is being sent upon the impulses of a carefully programed tape. As the result of several sessions lasting between fifteen and thirty minutes each, the ESP capability of such sensitives as Shawn Robbins and John Gaudry has markedly increased. Moreover, certain physical problems, such as headaches and poor eyesight, seem to have responded favorably to the treatment. I should add that all this is purely experimental and is being undertaken solely to determine what influence Dr. Baker's biomagnetic machine has upon ESP faculties.

The idea of increasing ESP in people through natural but carefully controlled means, such as the biomagnetic device just described, has apparently hit a responsive note with several American scientists as well. Dr. Harold Kenneth Fink, dean of the faculty and chairman of the Department of Psychobiology and Sociology at Fort Lauderdale College, Fort Lauderdale, Florida, has taught twenty-eight courses in ESP and related research subjects. He contacted me with a request for information concerning the results of my work with Dr. Baker's biomagnetic machine so that he could apply them in his own research activities. Other independent researchers have shown similar interest in this exciting new aspect of ESP research.

Unfortunately, some parapsychologists feel that disclosures should cover only areas in which absolute certainty exists concerning the nature of the phenomena, and since, in parapsychology, very few phenomena fall into that category, the number of such disclosures is not very large. This, I think, is an attitude caused by false fears that the public and the scientific community will look askance at disclosures if they tend to be revolutionary in nature. I have no such fears, nor do I have preconceived notions as to what may or may not be disclosed as long as I feel it is true, or at least reasonably likely to be true. I stand ready to correct my own views whenever that becomes necessary.

CHAPTER IX

ESP AND PHYSICAL PHENOMENA

Physical phenomena are those requiring some bodily action on the part of the medium or sensitive through whom the phenomenon takes place. They are also observable in the conventional way, and seem to rely upon energies drawn from living bodies, usually the body of the principal sitter or medium and others in the immediate vicinity. Physical phenomena include, first of all, deep trance mediumship, teleportation, or the movement of objects by mental powers, and materialization. In Professor Joseph Rhine's view, there are two main aspects of psychic phenomena: ESP and PSI. Dr. Rhine attributes the physical phenomena to the presence of the PSI force and calls the movement of objects due to mental efforts psychokinesis. In my own view, both ESP and the PSI force are aspects of one and the same force: in the ESP phenomenon, mental results are obtained by mental efforts, whereas in PSI phenomena physical results are obtained by mental effort. If, however, we consider the Einsteinian theory that mass and energy are but one and merely different aspects of the same force, then the difference between the two phenomena narrows down even more.

In the case of deep trance mediumship, the personality of the sensitive is temporarily displaced, voluntarily in most cases, and involuntarily on occasion, by the alleged personality of an outsider, usually a deceased person. There are also cases on record where incarnates may inhabit the physical body of a sensitive for the purpose of making a communication known, but the largest percentage of veridical cases of deep trance mediumship involves communication between a discarnate or dead person and a living being, the medium. In this case the medium serves merely as a channel of communication, allowing the discarnate entity to take over the speech mechanism of the medium's body without being involved in the communication in any way. As a matter of fact, one of the earmarks of genuine deep trance is the total lack of memory on the part of the medium, upon returning to full consciousness, as to what has transpired during the trance and as to what has come through his entranced lips. Partial trance is very common; in that case some memory remains.

Although full materialization depends primarily upon physical factors such as ectoplasm drawn from the physical medium as well as from the sitters to cover the mental projection from the other dimension, the very heart of the matter is certainly an ESP phenomenon. The materialized body of a discarnate is maintained only by the continuing ESP projection of its former self as remembered by the discarnate. The power to make this phenomenon possible is the same power used in the projection of the living personality. In fact, there is never any basic distinction to be made between psychic phenomena in the living person and in discarnate states; both techniques and underlying principles are exactly alike. This is so because the incarnate personality within the physical body

is identical with the latent etheric or spiritual body re-
leased to independence after physical death. In addition,
some ESP invariably plays a role in materialization séances in that the sitters and the medium, through their
extrasensory powers, sense a presence of discarnates in
the room. This is particularly so in the initial stages; once
full visible materialization has been accomplished, the
ESP phase is no longer necessary and generally ceases.
In a marginal way, ESP has been quite useful to the researchers with a degree of sensitivity who went to a number of American spiritualist camps to investigate so-called
materialization phenomena. In nearly all cases investigated they found fraud. Their inner feelings, another
term for intuitive processes, led them to suspect some of
the principals in these fraudulent sittings. In that respect
ESP is not used to communicate or make contact with
discarnates, but purely on a personal basis as an extension of the ordinary senses to gain additional knowledge.

The subject of teleportation is one that has fascinated
physical researchers for many years. Just as with materializations, fraud has certainly been practiced in this
field since teleportation represents a most difficult phase
of physical phenomena. Teleportation means the rapid
and seemingly instantaneous movement of a solid object
(or even a person) from one location to another without
the usual means of transport. A popular subdivision of
teleportation phenomena is called "apport," a term used
for the unexpected appearance or disappearance of solid
objects from either a person or a location. There is no
doubt in my mind that genuine apports exist and that the
power making such movement possible is essentially PSI

power, the physical force within man; whether the force is directed by an external entity or by part of the unconscious of the principal himself remains a debatable issue. Undoubtedly a number of verified cases exist where discarnate manipulation of apports is an undeniable fact. ESP enters the question of teleportation only in an indirect sense. The actual movement of the object is due to PSI, but the awareness and the understanding of the meaning of the process are realized by the recipient on the usual ESP "beam."

There is no other mode of communication available, except for the phenomenon of the so-called direct voice. This phenomenon, in which a human voice is heard independent of a medium and is an objective reality that can, among other things, be recorded on tape, requires the presence of a strong physical medium. Although in essence related to the informative form of mediumship represented by mental mediumship and ESP, direct voice phenomena are nevertheless classed as physical phenomena since a voice box is said to be constructed from invisible ectoplasm in order to make the phenomena possible at all. In the spiritualist séance rooms, especially of the 1920s, trumpets were used allegedly to increase the volume of such spirit voices. Frequently, the trumpets would float in the air without visible support and voices would indeed originate in them. Although a number of such séances have been unmasked as fraudulent, there is an equally impressive number of genuine occurrences where trumpets have indeed floated without trickery or means of wires. But the energies that are capable of maintaining a metal trumpet in the air for long periods of time and of producing human voices loud and obviously independent of the speech mechanism of an entranced medium are physical energies not properly of the ESP variety, at least not in the sense Professor Joseph Rhine would use the term. PSI and psychokinesis are very definitely physical phenomena, utilizing other aspects of the human personality and body than merely the mind. But I doubt very much that PSI forces could operate independently of ESP; ESP, on the other hand, can exist without the need for physical phenomena as expressed in psychokinesis.

Teleportation usually takes the form of inexplicable disappearances and reappearances of objects or sometimes total disappearance without reappearance. In the majority of cases on record there doesn't seem to be any rhyme or reason for these phenomena except perhaps as attention getters in a general sense. If we attribute teleportation to a split-off part of the personality of the subject himself, then we might explain it as unconscious ways of demanding attention or working out submerged frustrations. In German the general range of noisy and physical phenomena is referred to as a *poltergeist*. In my own view, however, poltergeist phenomena represent only the physical phase of regular hauntings or attempts at spirit communication, and are not phenomena by themselves, that is to say, caused independently by living people alone. Conventionally, such phenomena are connected with young people before the age of puberty who are present in the household, but that, too, is incorrect: the majority of cases do not concern youngsters at all but apply equally to older people, retarded individuals, and, if there is a common denominator among those who experience poltergeist phenomena, it seems to be people whose sexual lives are not fully expressed, leaving a residue of unused life-force within their bodies.

Some of the witnesses to phenomena of this kind are beyond suspicion, keen observers whose testimony is of much value.

Mrs. M. Ball is a practical nurse with special training in psychiatric work. She makes her home in the Middle West but has also spent much time in California. She is now close to sixty years old. From childhood on she has experienced a full range of ESP phenomena. Here is part of her report to me:

"Teleportation has been a nuisance to me all my life. Recently something of this nature happened to me which almost flattened me in surprise. On awakening from an afternoon nap, I found a greeting card on my chest. It was small in size with tulips and lilacs on the left side. It was printed in a foreign language and contained a verse from Matthew 5:3 (the language was Swedish.) My house is always locked with double locks. No one could possibly have entered. The card could have entered the house in a book or newspaper, but it could not have located itself on my chest without help.

"When I was in St. Louis in 1956, the keys to my bed-room and to the outside apartment door vanished almost while I was looking at them. I searched but found it impossible to locate them. I therefore could not get back into the apartment hotel in which I was staying and had to rent a room in a nearby rooming house. Three blocks away from my apartment hotel, in the rooming house, I placed my purse open on the bedside table and emptied it of all its contents. There was little in it to begin with. It was an inexpensive plastic purse without lining, with a

drawstring closing. While it was sitting open on my bedside table, I had the sudden desire to check it once more.
Just as I reached out to touch it, the keys fell with a klink,
obviously out of the air. I did not see them fall, but I certainly heard them.

"Four pages of a manuscript I had prepared at one
time in the hope of selling an article to a romance-type
magazine disappeared from the envelope on my dresser in
Riverside, California. This was in a new, uncluttered
room with no possibility of anyone entering. I had been
home all day on a Sunday, and late that afternoon I went
to make a final inspection of the manuscript in prepara-
tion for mailing it early the next day. I found the first four
pages missing. They had been in place late Saturday evening. I looked through everything in that room, but the
four pages simply were not found to be anywheres. Two
hours later I was standing at a metal-topped card table,
which was bare. Suddenly the pages, with an extra page
from some carbon copies I had not seen for weeks, were
lying on the table before my eyes. I had not seen them
transported through the air, nor did I see any movement
of any kind. They just materialized, face down, on the
clean card table. One moment it was empty, the next the
five pages of typed script were there miraculously."

The power that moved the keys and the manuscript was
of course PSI; but the intuitive processes that made Mrs.
Ball look in certain places or be near a spot where the
missing object would shortly be found is an ESP process,
utilizing mental channels.

Phenomena of this kind cannot be induced at will; a
state of expectancy can be produced if the subject is in-

clined toward physical phenomena. It would be wise to choose a quiet, not too bright room for the experiment, and to empty one's conscious mind of all extraneous thoughts. Once a state of repose is reached, the subject might project simple and direct requests for some proof that would tend to reinforce his own faith in physical phenomena. A request for a demonstration from one's unseen friends is sometimes answered and sometimes not. It helps if the subject is well rested, in excellent physical health, and not troubled by any problem or extensive worry. Total darkness in this type of phenomenon is probably advisable since physical phenomena do require it. But apports have also occurred in plain daylight. To be sure, not every mysterious disappearance of an object is due to psychic causes. People do forget or misplace things or allow themselves to be victimized by others without realizing it. But there are a sufficient number of cases, similar to the ones reported by Mrs. Ball, to warrant the statement that physical objects can be made to disappear spontaneously and reappear equally spontaneously in different locations. Whatever pattern of purpose emerges from these phenomena seems to indicate a dual reason: to prove that such phenomena are possible to begin with, and to call attention to the subject of the presence of some discarnate entity who wishes to be noticed, and possibly desires to work with the subject.

CHAPTER X

ESP IN TWINS, BLIND PEOPLE, AND DRUG ADDICTS

Unusual physical conditions have always had an impact upon the presence or absence of ESP capabilities. We are as yet not fully aware of the implications that certain birth defects may have on ESP. We do know that on occasion accidents can sharply increase the presence of ESP. A well-known case in point is the Dutch psychic Peter Hurkos, who had been a house painter plying his trade peacefully without giving any thought to extrasensory perception. One day he accidentally fell off a ladder and cracked his head. As a result of this shake-up, he began to predict future events with great accuracy. Eventually, his fame came to the attention of the Utrecht Center of Parapsychological Studies and he was asked to test as a psychic subject. From there he came to the attention of American researchers and eventually wound up in the employ of Henry Belk, amateur psychical researcher and part owner of the well-known Belk dry goods stores in the southern states. Mr. Belk tried to make good use of Hurkos' talents, including the use of them to discover thefts in his stores. However, Hurkos was restless with all this newly acquired fame and looked for greener pastures. Eventually, he wound up getting involved in the case of the Boston strangler, but due to politics, which he did not

understand at the time, he inadvertently caused difficulties between the Boston police and the district attorney.
In what appears to be a simple frame-up, Hurkos was
later arrested, and though the matter remained inconclusive, it left a blot on his personal record, a blot he did
not deserve. He moved to California, where he became
the protégé of motion-picture actor Glenn Ford, and currently employs his talents in private readings.

It is a well-known fact that twins represent a peculiar
situation, not only in relation to ESP talent, but also on a
more ordinary level. Twins often know of each other's
whereabouts intuitively; they tend to go through similar
experiences though widely separated in terms of distance,
and they frequently feel the same about individual causes
or people. This is not surprising since identical twins,
that is to say, those of the same sex who were born only
seconds apart and are the result of one divided ovum, are
in essence still connected on an etheric level even though
their physical bodies move apart from each other freely
and without seeming connection. But it would appear
from the evidence of paranormal material available that
identical twins continue to be connected very closely at
times in ways that suggest a common etheric body or at
any rate a continuing and close system of communication
between two halves of what must originally have been one
etheric body. This does not go as far as death of both
twins at the same time, but one twin frequently goes
through the death pangs of the other without being
aware of it taking place. Illnesses of one are quite frequently felt by the other, and symptoms can be observed
in one twin that actually belong to the other. These are

by no means produced by hysteria or because of fore-knowledge that the other twin is undergoing similar situations, but are produced quite innocently and involuntarily.

Marlene Rouse of California contacted me to make a statement concerning her ESP experiences and capabilities.

"I was born a twin, in fact, my ESP is so similar to your Dr. N. in your book *Predictions—Fact or Fallacy?* that I thought you might like to hear a little about me. [Dr. N., a California psychiatrist and medical doctor attached to a major hospital, who is also an identical twin, had reported a number of experiences between himself and his brother proving that both partook of psychic events at the same time.] As a twin I always thought of my sister as my other half, or part of me divided at birth. I therefore didn't think it strange that I knew what she was thinking, knew where she might be, and always be sick together. People didn't discuss ESP then, but I sensed my mother knew. Whenever my mother couldn't find my sister, she would call me and ask where she was. I always would take a guess and forget she even asked. As a child I was always the sick one, but my sister complained of the same symptoms. When I had a ruptured appendix, we argued over who was the sickest. When I was pregnant, she told me I was pregnant for she had had morning sickness, and as I telephoned the doctor to go to the hospital, my hand was still on the telephone when my mother called me telling me that my sister was complaining of labor pains.

"In October of 1963 I awoke in the middle of the morning with pains in my chest and arms. As a former student registered nurse, I knew the symptoms of a heart attack. I was rushed to the hospital for an examination. They found nothing wrong. While the doctor was examining me, the symptoms came again. He turned white and rushed out to do an EKG. The results were the most normal heart you could ever ask for. He passed the news to my doctor that I was faking. I then asked my sister if she was sick and she said that she hadn't been feeling well, but she didn't want to talk about it. For the next year I would be driving down towards the highway time after time and think what I would do if my twin sister would die. One night I woke up in the middle of the night gasping for breath with the same thought. On getting up, I saw my sister's light on and heard her gasping. I called her up and she denied it. Two weeks before her death, on the way to church, as I was driving towards this highway, that familiar feeling that I knew she was dead came again. Thoughts came such as, 'I just know she's dead, can't you drive any faster? Hurry! Darn, why did that car stop in our only path and block our way?' By this time, it was so real to me that I began to cry, speeding and acting out the real incident. Then I thought it was funny that there was no car in front of me when I complained of a car being stalled. As I passed the hospital turnoff, I stopped crying and thought of how silly I must be. When I arrived at church late, I immediately started running up the church steps, flung the swinging doors open, and felt like everyone turned and stared, but nobody did. It was such an odd feeling that my head dropped in dismay. I sat down next to my sister and stared at everything she was wearing, not believing that she was really alive. I kept thinking that she was wearing a new dress, but it wasn't new. I sobbed all through church and she kept asking me what was the matter, but I wouldn't tell. Later that day when I was with her at my mother's house, I asked my mother when she was going to buy the cemetery plot that she mentioned after my grandfather died. My sister usually cut in and thought me silly to discuss the matter, but not that day. She discussed her own feeling about how she would rather be buried. The following two weeks I tried to visit her every possible minute I could. During that time I saw that boney look on her face and said, 'You look dead even though I know you're alive.' She jumped out of her chair, calling me out for talking to her like that. In her rage, she blurted out something to the effect that she was the one who was really sick: not mother. I jumped up, saying, 'You're sick?' She clammed up, started breathing very fast, ordered me out of the house, claiming that her doctor didn't want her upset.

"On the night that she had the heart attack, my husband answered the phone. Because I was six months pregnant, they didn't want to tell me that she was dead on arrival until I got to the hospital. The thoughts I had had so vividly two weeks before came exactly as I had visioned. A car was stalled on the hospital turnoff in our way, which thus delayed our exit off the freeway. As I stopped the car at the hospital, I ran to find out if she were dead. As I flung open the swinging doors (as in the church), all the nurses did indeed turn to stare, wondering what to say to me. When one finally told me to go to the conference room, I dropped my head, knowing that this meant she was dead. As for the new dress incident, my sister stared at me in church on that last day of her life, for I was wearing a new dress that she hadn't seen before and she kept feeling the material and admiring it."

Frank Farnsworth has a twin brother named Francis. One brother lives in Florida, the other, in California. Mr. Farnsworth's report follows:

"We lived in a beat-up old brick house in the country in upstate New York. This particular late afternoon, my twin brother had gone to my aunt, Mrs. Lester Grant, for supper. I had wandered off into the woods and got lost. There was a distance of about twenty miles between my uncle's house and the old brick house in which we lived. It became dark, and I still couldn't find my way out of the woods. At this time, needless to say, I became frightened. I was almost ten years old. At the same time, my brother was sitting down to dinner at my uncle's house with the rest of the family when he began to cry. When he was asked what was wrong, he merely said, 'Something is wrong with Frank.' Eventually, I found my way out of the woods and came home. By this time my grandmother was quite upset over my whereabouts."

Experiments conducted by Professor H. N. Banerjee, Indian parapsychologist, and by others have shown that people deprived of their ordinary senses sometimes develop a keener ESP capability. In particular does this hold true for blind people whether they are blind from birth or by accident. Some years ago a Canadian psychic demonstrated her ability to drive through the streets of a major city blindfolded because, she claimed, she could see the road just as well with her eyes closed. The police, not very understanding in matters of ESP, arrested her for driving in a manner that would endanger the lives of the population. But the psychic demonstrated her ability in court and got off free. That, of course, was not true blindness but simulated blindness to make a point. Similar experiments have recently been conducted in Russia by blindfolding sensitives; messages were read in books, objects were described, and "the inner eyes" used as if they were physical eyes. There is no doubt that man can train himself to use other organs to take the place of eyesight. Various researchers have proved that any sensitive surface of the body, from fingertips to elbows, can be used to transmit information to the sight center in the brain. With patience and training, such substitute organs can almost simulate the sight of human eyes. Almost any psychic, with his eyes closed, can give accurate descriptions of places, whether where he is or at a distance. All this suggests that there is a duplicate set of eyes in the make-up of man, just as there are duplicate organs for other functions. Since the etheric body is a complete duplicate of the physical body, although more sensitive than the latter, it stands to reason that it contains eyes as well. It is with those eyes that the blind see.

L. Donn of Pennsylvania reports the story of a blind chemist who lived at a hotel in New Jersey in the years 1960–1964. The chemist had been blinded in an accident in his laboratory and had taken to sitting in the lobby of the hotel by himself, telling those who would listen what was going on in the various rooms of the hotel. Many confirmed that the chemist could indeed "see" what was going on in their rooms.

The question of drugs and ESP goes back to the beginning of public discussion of drug-taking, when Aldous

Huxley recommended mescalin as a desirable way of opening the door to the unconscious. Undoubtedly, drugs have been taken since the beginning of time, but in terms of modern scientific observance we are dealing with perhaps the last twenty or twenty-five years. When mescalin was followed by lysergic acid ⚹113, later known as LSD, and in turn by peyote, the drug of the Indians, the field seemed wide open for experimentation with various drugs, especially those called "hallucinogens." Dr. Andrija Puharich, in his book *The Sacred Mushroom*, was the first to discuss the relationship between certain drugs and ESP experiences. Celebrated mediums like Eileen Garrett and others decided to experiment with drugs under strictly controlled conditions and with the supervision of their psychiatrists. As yet, the full impact of the drug scene had not dawned upon mankind. It was a novelty, something the avant-garde did, and was said to produce far-out sensations. As the years went on, the dangers of drug-taking became apparent. Those mediums who had taken even small amounts of LSD in the hope of having extraordinary psychic experiences became ill and had to discontinue even so slight a use as they had subjected themselves to. Doctors were as yet divided concerning the dangers of drug-taking, some saying that only the heavier drugs were habit-forming and damaging to body and mind, while "grass," or marijuana, was not. Today there are very few doctors who will omit even marijuana from their lists of undesirable drugs, since the results are cumulative, and may not show for many years.

From the psychical research point of view and my own conviction, drug-taking is utterly useless. Not only does it cause serious disorientation in the long run, if not indeed in a shorter period, but the results obtained under drugs do not seem to be related to any kind of reality remotely comparable to the realities of genuine ESP experiences. I have gone into this in greater detail in a recent work entitled *Psycho-Ecstasy*, in which I suggested that ESP and its variants were a better way of getting "high" than the taking of drugs, and gave certain techniques leading to that desirable state. True, the fantasies encountered under the influence of hallucinogenic drugs, especially LSD, seem to suggest an entering into the higher realms of consciousness. True, the visions described by those experiencing them under those conditions have the width and scope of extraordinary spiritual encounters, but the material thus obtained is artificial and due solely, in my opinion, to the altered chemical state of the bloodstream in the subject. Mental imagery is largely controlled by the delicate chemical balance in the bodily system. When alien substances, such as hallucinogenic drugs, are injected into the system, they produce altered states of consciousness. While these altered states may mimic authentic states of bliss or even ecstasy, they are nevertheless due to interference from outside agents rather than due to genuine contact with another dimension.

D.H. is a twenty-six-year-old resident of one of the eastern states, son of an attorney in a small town, who was educated in Catholic schools until the eighth grade. Later he attended a liberal college and studied for a master's degree in library science. Although raised a Catholic, he eventually turned agnostic. Scientifically oriented, the young man was given to inventions and hoped to make a living as an inventor. Mr. H., in addition, is a young man totally honest about himself. In a statement given to me about his ESP experiences, he says:

"I am a heavy drinker and used to stand first in drinking in a college of six hundred students. I still do pretty good, but I can't drink like I used to. I've had lots of sex and three affairs. During three semesters I experimented with drugs, grass, Dexedrine and methadone, and LSD. I've only had acid three times, and that was the only one which I liked, and I would take it more often if I were certain that it did not produce mutations. I've had no drugs since April of 1968."

His scientific bent did not satisfy him entirely, and he kept searching for some evidence that his scientific mind could accept concerning an afterlife. Until that time he thought that psychic phenomena did not exist.

"Then, in May of 1967, I took acid for the first time. I had the greatest time of my life, and the following day, in a period of about an hour, I underwent a change which caused me to throw away a dime's worth of grass, to stop living with a girl I had been living with because I then considered our relationship to be too superficial; life became very meaningful to me, I became very relaxed, and I looked upon my body as integrated, whereas before I considered it to be a mind attached to what is below my head. I started to study hard and I gave up excessive drinking. The effect lasted for about three months, and then mostly left me except for the fact that I have never gone back to excessive drinking.

"In April of 1968, at a time when I had been dropping about thirty milligrams of Dexedrine a day, but not taking any other drugs, I sort of fell in love with a girl whom I had seen in the Dining Commons. She looked interested, but we did not meet. That night I went to bed and all of a sudden I started sending out brain waves, for lack of a better word. I thought I was imagining it, but I could send waves from my brain in a steady stream. They seemed to be circling around and gradually extending out farther and farther. After perhaps five minutes, they stopped circling, and wavered back and forth in the direction of a girl's dormitory, where the above-mentioned girl lived. Then the waves stopped wavering and were steady in one direction for perhaps half an hour, after which they went away and I was able to go to sleep. I thought that all of this had been in my head, but the next day, when I went to lunch, a strange girl came over to my table, sat down, glared at me and said, 'My roommate wants you to stop sitting on her head.' The experience scared me, for I did not know what was happening. But the same thing happened again every day for the next week and a half. I had little control over what was happening except for one night when I was able to prevent these waves from establishing contact with another mind. On one occasion I was tuned into someone else in another dormitory. In this instance there was no exchange of information, but it felt sort of like completely possessing a girl, more so than in sex."

I am frequently asked about ESP in children. I find that children up to the age of four or five are quite often psychic and can describe situations, scenes, or give the names of people they couldn't possibly know. There are cases of young children speaking in the voice of an adult, reporting in great and authentic detail experiences they could not possibly have had. However, some of this may be due to reincarnation memories that later fade. There seems to be a period between ages five and eight when such occurrences recede, only to return after the age of puberty. There is nothing particularly frightening about ESP in children, provided it is handled sensibly by the parents. One should neither deny the fact that the child has an unusual experience nor particularly encourage his dwelling upon it. Rather the parents should point out that ESP is a perfectly natural ability in man and gently encourage the child to talk about it with them.

Mrs. J.H. and her family live in one of the southern states. Mrs. H. has for a long time been interested in psychical research and has kept a record of her son L.J.'s ESP experiences. It is noteworthy that both parents have also had extensive ESP experiences of various kinds. The husband is a retired Navy man serving as a town policeman, and L.J. was four years old at the time of the reported incident.

One night the child would not go off to sleep but instead demanded that his mother come to his bedside. He had something to tell her. "This house is crooked. It's going to fall down." What could the mother do but assure him that God would look after them all? So he finally went off to sleep. However, the statement aroused her curiosity. When they had moved into the house, they had noticed that the hardwood floor in the living-room closet did not meet the wall. It had not occurred to her then that this could mean the house was indeed crooked. A week later, the boy still spoke of the house falling down, and asked God not to let it fall on him. A few days later he put his arms around a tree in the front of the house, then came over to his mother, and said, "That tree is going to fall down too." Mrs. H. asked some questions about their house and discovered that it was built over a major fault and that scientists indeed expected a major earthquake within the next few years.

CHAPTER XI

ESP AND TELEPATHY

"It must be telepathy," the astonished person exclaims
when someone has just "read his mind." Erroneously referred to by the public as "mental telepathy," telepathy
signifies communication from mind to mind without
recourse to sensory perception. The transfer of thoughts
from one mind to another is accomplished at great speed
and almost no loss in time. There is a tiny fraction of
time—elapsed time, that is—between the transmission of a
thought or image and its reception on the other end in another mind, but the amount of elapsed time is so insignif-
icantly small that, for all practical purposes, we can say
that telepathy is an instant transmission of thoughts from
one person to another. It works best in times of stress and
when ordinary communications are down. It is particularly strong between people who have an emotional
bond, such as relatives, friends, lovers, or people who in
some fashion rely one upon the other. The instances of
mothers feeling the distress of a child, at a distance of
course, are literally numerous; cases where someone just
has to get through to another person and uses his mind to
send forth a message are equally numerous and are well
attested in the files of most reputable psychical research

societies, such as the American Society for Psychical Research.

Stress telepathy, however, is by no means the only way of communicating mind to mind. To a degree, telepathy can be induced experimentally as well. In experimental telepathy, sender and receiver should know each other in order to make the contact possible. It is extremely difficult to send out a thought message to someone you cannot visualize. By knowing the receiver, or potential receiver, no evidential material is being given away since the message itself contains the evidence. It is immaterial whether the two parties are close by, such as in two different rooms in one and the same apartment, or whether they are a thousand miles away one from the other: telepathy does not recognize any difference. It is, however, important that both sender and receiver be in a calm state of mind, in good physical health, and comfortable. Noise and other distractions tend to interfere with the possible transmission. It is advisable to transmit, or try to transmit, relatively simple messages or thoughts. These may be sentences or they may be visual impressions, such as definite scenes. In a way, this resembles the card test devised by Professor Joseph Rhine at Duke University except that, instead of artificial symbols, real ideas and scenes are being used for transmission. Also, sender and receiver are not merely separated by a piece of cardboard, creating an artificial wall between them, but are literally apart and cannot see each other. Telepathy works a little like radio: small impulses, specifically programed by the sender, are sent out to a known receiver; the receiver, in turn, decodes the message and allows his conscious mind to formulate it into words. Telepathy works equally well between living people and between incarnates and discarnates. However, experimentally speaking, adequate proof can be obtained only from telepathy between living individuals. Those wishing to try their hand at telepathy and who have a suitable partner should plan on regular sessions of perhaps half an hour each during which a number of ideas or images are transmitted. A record should be kept on each end as to what is being sent and what is being received. Afterward the two should be compared and scored. Anything considerably above the so-called law of average is significant. Generally speaking, if a receiver identifies three out of ten possible messages fully or nearly so, he will have breached the law of average and scored in ESP. It is unlikely that ten out of ten are ever received. Some messages may be obscured in part or they may be received out of sequence, for some strange reason. Thought transference is outside the conventional time stream; therefore, the sequence can be jumbled, since all messages sent are coexistent in the timeless dimension.

While the incentive of experimentally induced telepathy furnishes the emotional motivation so necessary for success, necessity is a much stronger inducing agent. When ordinary communication is impossible and the initiator of the telepathic message realizes this, forces are brought into play that make the message very strong. This may be in real crisis situations or it may be in only comparatively unimportant domestic or personal matters. As long as there is an element of urgency and the realization that there is no other avenue to get through, telepathy may indeed succeed. For the latter type of telepathic communication, I can cite an example of my own. One Saturday afternoon my wife had gone to her doctor's and

I was home alone working. Suddenly I realized she would be near a specialty shop where a certain type cheese I liked very much was being sold. I could not disturb her while she was at the doctor's for an examination, and I knew that she would leave immediately upon its completion. The best I could hope for was that she would telephone me. I did not concentrate on this but merely held the thought of her calling me on her own to inquire about my cheese. I knew that she would be at the doctor's at four o'clock. One minute after four the telephone rang. It was my wife, saying, "You want me to get some cheese, don't you?" I had not discussed cheese with her that day at all.

The famous Australian explorer Sir Hubert Wilkins and the Little Rock, Arkansas, psychic Harold Sherman conducted what amounts to classical experiments in telepathy during Sir Hubert's travels to the North Pole. He was to transmit information about himself daily from the Arctic, Sherman was to take down whatever he received, and the material would then be compared after Sir Hubert came back to New York. A team of researchers stood by whenever Sherman was getting messages telepathically. This happened in a New York hotel room under test conditions. On one such occasion, Harold Sherman insisted that he saw, that is, telepathically, Sir Hubert Wilkins dancing in evening clothes. This seemed particularly improbable since at the time the explorer was due at the Arctic base of his expedition. But when Sir Hubert returned to New York and the matter was brought up, the following developed. En route to his Arctic base, his plane had been forced down in a snowstorm and had landed at Calgary, the capital of the Canadian province of Alberta. Such a dignitary as Sir Hubert naturally brought out top people in government to greet him. It so happened that the governor of Alberta was being inaugurated that day, and shortly after Sir Hubert's unscheduled arrival, the inauguration ball took place. Naturally, the governor invited his distinguished guest to come and, since Sir Hubert had no evening clothes of his own, lent him a suit to wear. Thus what Harold Sherman saw thousands of miles away in New York was indeed correct.

Mrs. Marlene Rouse of California, an identical twin of whom I have spoken in an earlier chapter, reported an interesting incident of telepathy where urgency was a motivating factor:

"One day I visited my grandfather and he looked so boney in the face that I was sure he was dying. I called my mother to tell her to visit him as he didn't look as if he were going to live. She went to see him and scolded me for scaring her. My grandfather went to the hospital and when my mother visited him she said that he looked so well that she went to Lake Tahoe for the weekend. She did not tell me where she would stay, but my grandfather did die, and I called her long distance, and had her paged in every casino I could think of. At about eight o'clock in the evening I gave up. I closed my eyes in tears, saying, 'Mom, where are you?' All of a sudden my thoughts said, 'Blackjack.' I immediately thought, 'Oh no. She is winning. That means she won't come home for at least a couple of days.' I kept saying, 'Please lose so you'll come home,' for about fifteen minutes. Then I felt so exhausted that I gave up. I went to her house and left a note asking her to call me immediately.

"During the night my mother did call me, saying that she was staying at a hotel called Blackjack and was playing blackjack, winning, when all of a sudden between 8:00 and 8:15 P.M. she started losing every single hand. She couldn't believe that for fifteen minutes she couldn't win at least one hand, so she said that her luck had turned so badly that she went back to her paid room, and didn't even want to stay the night if her luck was that bad. I thought that God had answered my prayers, for I had never heard of telepathy."

J.S. is a Cleveland-born college graduate currently making her home in California. All her life she has had ESP experiences, but the incident of particular interest here indicates a form of telepathy somewhat different from both experimentally induced telepathy and spontaneous urgency telepathy. This particular form of communication is between the unconscious mind of a sleeping person and the conscious mind of a person who is fully awake. Here is her report:

"I remember vividly when I was in college that on one occasion I went to the library for I was doing some research. Suddenly I heard my friend Brian call my name. Thinking he might have come to the library, I looked around for him but I could not find him. Then I heard him call my name again, as though he were standing next to me, and asked if he could come in. I looked, and I realized that Brian was not in the library. I then looked at the time, and when I came home I found Brian on the couch asleep. When I walked in, he asked me where I had been. I told him and asked him in return where he had been at 2:00 P.M., the time when I had the experience at the library. He replied he had just gotten off work about one o'clock and had come over to see if there was anyone home at our house. He had called my name outside the house, but when no one answered he opened the door, called again, asked if he could come in. No one was home, so he laid down on the couch."

Nearly everyone familiar with recent developments in parapsychology and ESP research knows of the amazing experiments undertaken by Dr. Jules Eisenbud of Colorado with the Chicago bellhop Ted Serios. Mr. Serios can project into a camera or television tube images of objects or scenes thousands of miles away. He does this with his mind, not using any artificial means of projection. The authenticity of this process is well established and further experimentation with Mr. Serios is going on at this time. A number of universities have used his services as a subject in order to study the possibility of thought transference under controlled conditions. There are those who feel that Serios projects images by a process similar to telepathy. Judging from the material that I've examined, however, both in the book *The World of Ted Serios* and that shown to me by Professor Robert Jeffries of the University of Bridgeport, Connecticut, I feel that astral projection and rapid transmission of thoughts while at the destination may account for at least part of the images obtained. Since some of the Serios material pertains not only to distant places but also to distances in time, and since the view indicates a very high observation point at times, it seems to me that Mr. Serios is able to project part of himself as an observer and report back to his conscious mind, in some as yet not fully understood fashion, what he sees at a distance in both time and space. The process therefore seems to be more complicated than simple telepathy.

Lastly, I would like to point out that so-called stage mentalists who claim to read a person's mind are almost never doing this. The majority of mentalists are clever entertainers, whether they use stooges in the audience or not. Occasionally, some genuine ESP is involved, but the entertainer is most likely the first one to deny this. There is no evidence that anyone can read another person's mind. There is, however, evidence that a person's thoughts can be caught by another person if the reader is close by. But this is somewhat like reading the record, since material from the person's past is generally also involved. "Mind reading" is not telepathy.

CHAPTER XII

THE NATURE OF TIME AND ESP

One of the most puzzling problems with ESP projections
into the so-called future remains unresolved in terms of
orthodox science: how can facts that are not in existence
at the time they are being described by a person with
ESP, how can people who may not have been born yet at
the time when someone describes and names them, be
squared with the conventional view concerning the sequence of events and the time–space continuum? The
past is followed by the present, which in turn is followed
by the future. The sequence cannot be reversed, nor can
anyone jump from the past into the future without dwelling in the present.

Against this view stand thousands upon thousands of
verified cases where people have foreseen future events in
great detail long before these events became objective
reality without having any clues as to the events themselves. Thousands of cases, which do not allow an alternate explanation of either coincidence or vagueness or
guesswork, are available to serious researchers in the files
of reputable research societies. Foretelling the future in
detail is not an isolated instance of some extraordinarily
gifted individual; it is a fairly common occurrence among
many types of individuals, young and old, rich and poor,

living in almost every country on earth. It has occurred in the past, and it continues to occur daily. It is, in fact, a natural part of human personality that some individuals can foresee future events. It is not the same with everyone, to be sure, but allowing for degrees of perfection, the ability to break through the time and space barrier is inherent in the nature of man.

In an earlier chapter dealing with clairvoyance and other forms of divination, I have already cited examples of a specific nature. Since the facts are amply supported by evidence, we must find a scientific edifice which fits the existing conditions rather than continue to try to force paranormal occurrences of this kind into the existing laws of science. They simply do not fit. When the facts require a re-evaluation of older laws, then these laws must be revised to fit the facts; otherwise, science becomes a living lie. Assuming, then, that foreseeing the future is to a large extent a natural phenomenon inherent in every individual, our view concerning the nature of time is incorrect. There must be an explanation as to why people with ESP can leave the time stream temporarily, stick their heads outside of it, as it were, to look into the so-called future or into the past, and come up with information they could not consciously know. The only logical explanation for this phenomenon is the existence of a timeless dimension where events are stationary, preordained in general terms, and put there by a variety of circumstances, chiefly a very involved and sophisticated law of cause and effect far beyond what we, in the physical world, call law of cause and effect. If events are stationary, then we are in motion toward them. When we meet up with a specific event, the event occurs to us. At that point, we have a

number of alternatives: we can either ignore it; we can
run from it; or we can move toward it positively, actively.
Depending upon our initiative at this point, one of several
consequences will result, leading, in turn, to a new set of
events in the distance. The East Indian philosophers
called this the "law of karma."

I have already given testimony to the authenticity of
reincarnation material in an earlier book called *Born
Again: The Truth About Reincarnation,* and find that reincarnation is the only logical way to accept the seeming
injustices and irrelevancies of ordinary life. There is a
link between each and every one of us, a deeper meaning
to every event in our lives, no matter how insignificant it
appears on the surface, and a lesson to be learned. Karmic
law is beyond the law of cause and effect, even beyond
the law of meaningful coincidence or acausal synchronicity
of Carl Jung: it is the Universal Law that governs not only
our lives but the world, both material and immaterial.
ESP is used to implement karmic law; the situations that
confront us from time to time are not irrevocable. Some
situations are only warnings and can be altered by conscious effort. Others are predestined fate situations and
cannot be altered, but we are given advance notice of
them to prepare us for the event. The means by which we
overcome the limitations of the ordinary five senses is, of
course, ESP. That much the karmic law permits us; anything within us at our disposal, be it natural in the ordinary sense or supernatural in the way the word is used by
those other than I, may be brought out and used for the
purpose of improving our lot. Those who cannot use ESP
because they are not aware of their abilities, or who
choose to ignore it, will bear the full brunt of events

when and if they occur; those who are fortunate enough to be aware of their ESP talents and know how to use them, or at least to accept them, will be that much ahead in the game of life.

ESP in relation to reincarnation and karma is the gentle awareness of greater forces at play than one's own. It is the feeling of being maneuvered, of being pushed in certain directions so that one may react in certain ways without being forced to do so. It is the realization of links, why one meets a certain person and the understanding of what this meeting means in terms of future action. The most important thing, whenever you meet a new person, is to find out what is meant to be done between you, for the encounter is never accidental or without some form of hoped-for action. Discovering what the positive action should be in each and every case may not be easy, but it is the way in which we are being tested by karmic law and given the opportunity to perform well.

Whenever you have the feeling that "fate" is at work, a sense of destiny, a tingling sensation indicating that you had better pay attention to things that are happening around you, or if a new acquaintance makes a deep impression on you, you should use your ESP abilities to discover what the next step ought to be. Following your intuition in such cases may run counter to logic, even to society's rules at times, but it may very well be the proper answer to the karmic pattern laid out for you by a superior power.

Barbara M. is in her early twenties and lives in California. She consulted me concerning visions of people she has had in dreams, only to meet these people, strangers to her at the time of her dream, several days later. She did not understand how it was possible for her to see such faces in the dream state when there was no objective reason for her to have the impressions. Inevitably, she met them several days or weeks later. On one occasion, she questioned a person about having had a mustache at one time because she had seen him with a mustache in her dream. Puzzled, the man admitted that he had shaved off his mustache a short time before.

But the case that more than anything else made Barbara wonder about her ESP experiences indicated a certain interplay of her ESP with the hands of destiny. Here is her report:

"About three years ago some of my friends decided to drive up to the coast. We were about twenty-five or thirty miles from town when I felt that something terrible would happen to us if we went much farther. I insisted that we go back. They asked why, and I told them that if we went much farther, we would be involved in an automobile accident. The next day I read in the newspaper of an accident not more than a few miles from where we had turned around. It happened approximately five minutes after we had turned around. Both cars involved were totally wrecked, all the people, about six, were killed instantly. The next day we decided to check out a rather morbid idea. We tested to see if we would have been involved in the accident. We drove at the same speed, same traffic conditions, etc. Had we gone on, it was determined that we too would have been involved in the accident."

In this example, which is rather typical of this type of phenomenon, the other cars were already on the so-called time track, racing for a rendezvous with death. The third party, in this case Barbara M.'s car, was also set on a collision course with the other two, but because Barbara has ESP, she sensed the event before coming to it. Recognizing her ESP hunch and acting upon it, which are two different things, she made a positive decision, that is, positive from her point of view, and was saved. In instances of this kind, ESP is used not to foresee actual events, but the tendency toward certain events at a point where individuals can still do something about them as far as their participation in them is concerned.

ESP TEST SHEETS

1. If you wish to determine whether you (and others) have basic ESP capabilities, sit in the same room but at least two or three yards distant from other people. At a given signal, concentrate *lightly* on any numeral between one and ten. For about thirty seconds hold the thought of that numeral and visualize it being written on a piece of paper at the same time. Close your eyes when you do this, then open them and look directly at the proposed receiver of your message. Pause for a moment, then do the same thing with another numeral until you have done it with five different numerals. At the same time, the proposed receiver has been instructed to write down whatever numeral he gets mentally. When the experiment is completed, compare notes, since you yourself have also written down the sequence of numerals to be broadcast mind to mind. We find that two out of five is not unusual, three out of five may occur, and four out of five is most unusual. Frequently, the sequence of numerals broadcast may be inverted or numerals may be received out of sequence. I have already explained earlier in this book that this is due to the fact that telepathy works in a non-time, non-space dimension where all things, all thoughts, co-exist simultaneously.

2. Testing for ESP capabilities with images, sentences, or visualizations of thoughts. The same method as in test number one is to be employed, except that an entire sentence is being broadcast or a visual concept is being sent out. Make sentences short, though, and visual concepts fairly simple, as it may be difficult to hold the thought of a very complicated image or a very long sentence for the time required for it to be received.

(a) First sentence (image) broadcast

(b) Second sentence (image) broadcast

(c) Third sentence (image) broadcast

Result:

First sentence (image) received 1. completely 2. partially 3. not at all

Second sentence (image) received 1. completely 2. partially 3. not at all

Third sentence (image) received 1. completely 2. partially 3. not at all

Remarks:

ESP REPORT SHEET

Those wishing to report a spontaneous phenomenon or controlled experimental incident involving ESP may do so by filling in the spaces listed below. If you wish, you may send a copy of this report sheet to me care of the publisher of this book.

Name:

Address:

Telephone number(s):

Occupation of person reporting incident:

2. Place and time of incident:

3. Nature of incident:

4. Witnesses to incident, with full names, addresses, telephone numbers, and occupations:

5. My own interpretation of the incident reported is as follows:

Those among my readers who wish to learn more about ESP and parapsychology in general may wish to read some of the books available on the subject. A recent book of mine entitled *The Handbook of Parapsychology*, and an earlier work, *ESP and You*, as well as the works of Louisa Rhine, of Professor Joseph B. Rhine, and of Harold Sherman will be found useful.

Those interested in joining the American Society for Psychical Research, which has an extensive library and sponsors lectures, will find that this is possible without difficulty and that the society is listed in the New York City telephone directory.

The Association for Research and Enlightenment has branches throughout the United States and headquarters at Virginia Beach, Virginia. It is also known as the Edgar Cayce Foundation and has an interesting and many-sided program.

Finally, the American Society for the Occult Sciences, of which I am the research director, is a membership society with a newsletter dealing primarily with ESP phenomena. It can be contacted at 227 East Forty-fifth Street, New York, N.Y. 10017.

I teach classes in parapsychology, including an ESP

workshop, at the New York Institute of Technology, 888 Seventh Avenue, New York, N.Y. 10019. Inquiries should be directed to the Director of Admissions of the Evening School.

Mail from those wishing to report actual incidents, fully documented and with all data furnished, will be received by me either through my publisher or the New York Institute of Technology address. A stamped, self-addressed return envelope must accompany such reports. Questions or inquiries concerning this field cannot be answered individually, but cases worthy of further attention will be dealt with in due time and as opportunity permits.